PRAISE FOR PEAK SELF-CONTROL

Accessibly written, this is a well-crafted self-help book offering advice to people who want to achieve their goals but often don't have the willpower to do it.

— WISHING SHELF

I like the concept and Said Hasyim tackles the topic methodically and also from a psychological point of view.

— READERS' FAVORITE

PEAK SELF-CONTROL

BUILDING STRONG WILLPOWER TO
ACCOMPLISH IMPORTANT GOALS

SAID HASYIM

Edited by
DAVID ARETHA

For you

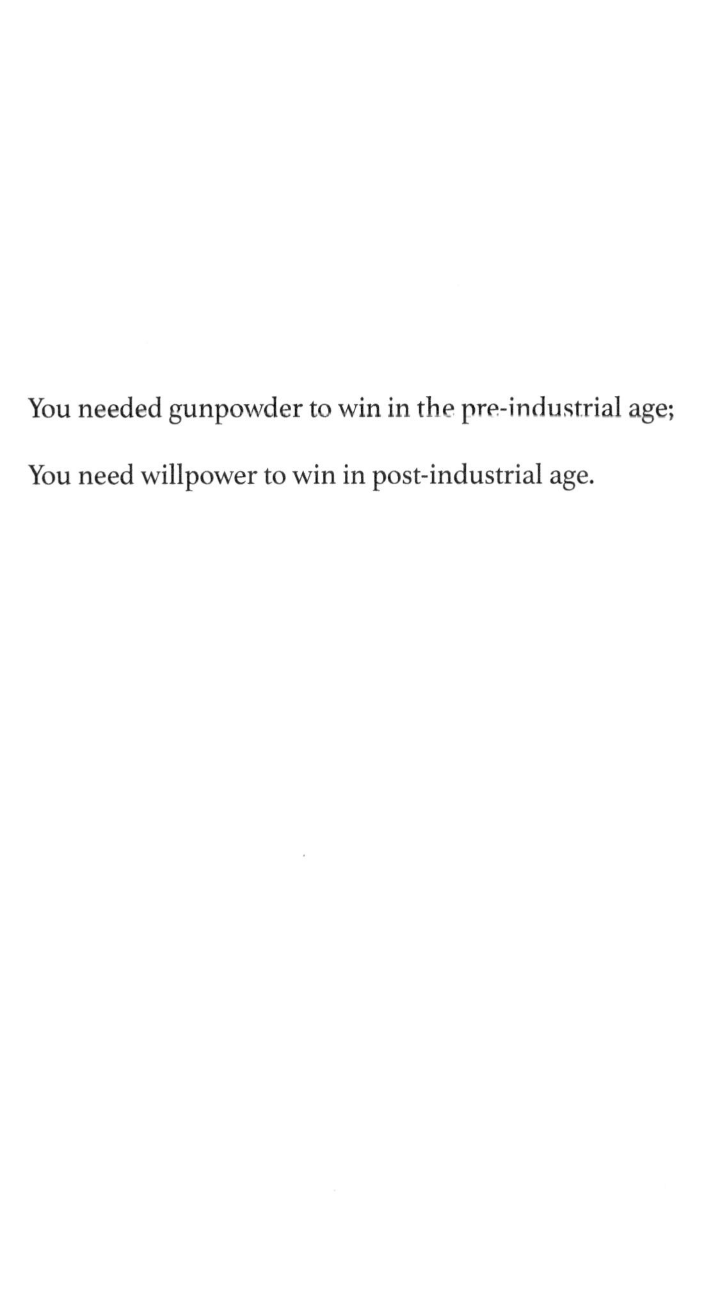

You needed gunpowder to win in the pre-industrial age;

You need willpower to win in post-industrial age.

CONTENTS

DISCLAIMER

This book contains advice and information relating to health care. It should be used to supplement rather than replace the advice of your doctor or another trained health professional. If you know or suspect you have a health problem, it is recommended that you seek your physician's advice before embarking on any medical program or treatment. All efforts have been made to assure the accuracy of the information contained in this book as of the date of publication. The author disclaims liability for any medical outcomes that may occur as a result of applying the methods suggested in this book.

INTRODUCTION

It was the 31ˢᵗ of December, and you committed yourself to five New Year's resolutions: wake up early, exercise, quit smoking, swear off junk food, and learn the violin. You told yourself, "How hard can they be? I just need to plan my schedule; I have the same twenty-four hours as other people who made it." You started practicing them in the new year, as did many other people with their own resolutions.

Day 1:

You woke up early with the alarm and were exuberant to hit the gym. On your way home, you saw some people smoking, but ignored them. You resolved not to touch cigarettes again. You sniffed the aroma of your favorite juicy burger from the nearby restaurant. Resisting the temptation, you reminded yourself not to think about it. Upon reaching home, you prepared a bowl of oatmeal, sprinkled with blueberries, and ate that. The taste has never appealed to you, but you force-fed yourself. While washing the dish, you saw a bag of potato chips in your cupboard, but you stayed committed to your pledge and wouldn't eat that. So far so good. You had risen early, gone to the gym, had not smoked, and had not eaten junk food. The urge to smoke came sometimes, but, heaven forbid, you knew you were strong and would not give in.

It was time to learn violin, so you took out the violin stashed in your garage, then browsed for violin lessons online. The thirty minutes' duration of the course discouraged you. You put the online course on hold and promised to look at it later. It was nighttime, and the urge to smoke got stronger, and your craving for donuts intensified. You stuck to your regimen and ate a salad for dinner.

After dinner, you realized that you had not ticked "learning violin" on your to-do checklist. You postponed doing it until the next day, giving an excuse to yourself that you had been lifting hard in the gym today. You summarized that your day had been perfect and that you did all these well, then you hurried to bed before the devil inside you prodded you with more temptations.

While lying on your bed, your temptation to smoke was exacerbated, and your growling stomach was hungry for the spicy instant noodles. You convinced yourself that it was okay to just eat the instant noodles and smoke just one cigarette. You assured yourself that you would stick to your new routine the next day. After all, you had completed a meritorious deed by waking up early and going to the gym earlier in the day.

You rushed to the kitchen to boil a pan of water to cook two packs of instant noodles. While waiting for the water to boil, you drew a cigarette from the pack on your desk and lit it up. After smoking, you satisfied your voracious appetite for instant noodles and comforted yourself by saying that you deserved it after the hard gym session in the morning.

Day 2:

The alarm clock rang early in the morning, but you were still very sleepy. Therefore, you went back to sleep with an excuse that your muscles deserved more rest from yesterday's session. You then woke up at 8 a.m. and skipped the gym. At the office, you dealt with a demanding boss and had a tight deadline. You gave yourself another excuse to smoke a cigarette and promised you would stop the next day.

Reaching home hungry, you felt as if you hadn't eaten a burger for a lifetime, which justified your purchase of a double cheeseburger. You promised it would be the last time.

Day 17:

Nothing seemed to work. You still struggled to wake up early, and you couldn't find time to go to the gym. You needed the cigarette to do well at work. There was no point to eat clean since you were still fat. It would take a long time to learn violin, and you thought it wasn't worth your time. In despair, you ended these mainstream fad habits as you lost your resolve. Perhaps you just didn't have the time, or it was your genetic flaw that you were born this way, you convinced yourself. Anyway, most of your friends were the same too. This was the consolation message you gave to yourself.

Does this story resonate with you? If yes, you are not alone, and it is not your genetic defects that fail you. A survey conducted by Statista in 2018 showed that only 4% of Americans stuck to their New Year's resolution.[1] The most important culprit of this is **willpower usage.** An American Psychological Association survey in 2011 found that lack of **self-control** is the top reason people fail in achieving their commitments.[2]

Many years ago, while venturing into my personal project to maximize time use and productivity, I fixed and synergized my body's clock as a baseline to plan my activities and get the most out of my day. In this modern world filled with an inconceivable number of distractions, gaining high self-control becomes more crucial to set up any new habit and work at your best. This book compiles all the empirical experiments that I have learned on willpower use for over five years. Applying the strategies has helped me to fulfill more tasks and add a few more life-changing habits into my already-packed schedule. I reached a point that I needed to remove some good routines that I had cultivated, or else I risked disrupting the balance of other areas of my life. At the time of writing this, I have practiced the following habits daily on top of my 9-5 office job:

- Waking up before sunrise and without alarm
- Time-restricted fasting
- Physical exercising
- Gratitude journaling
- Self-appreciation journaling
- Self-affirmation journaling

- Learning a foreign language
- Reading books
- Brain exercising
- Writing books (during weekend only)

Because of the limited hours that I have in a day, I had to choose and prioritize only the habits that brought the most positive outcomes to my life. I mention this not to brag about what I do, but to prove to you that if an average Joe like me can build these habits, so can you. And, by the way, I do this with joy, and I would be most grateful to add more if I had just an extra one hour a day.

In this book, we will go through common willpower use, how to reduce its usage, how to replenish it, and even how to increase its reserve. We will also discuss how to detect weakened willpower, how to handle the relapse when you encounter willpower failure, and practical willpower planning that you can adopt daily.

This book will not discuss the mythical "whenever there is a will, there is a way" kind of willpower that you can command at will. It lays out the genuine science behind it and what you can do to translate the science into practical actions that can help you optimize your willpower.

No one is immune to problems that willpower depletion causes, not even the high-ranking officers, CEOs, heads of states, religious leaders, or global figures. In fact, they are *the most vulnerable*, yet few people are aware of this. When they deplete their willpower, they lose their usual grit to make a good decision, which could lead to regrettable actions.

1
———

WHAT IS WILLPOWER?

 Welcome, Homo Sapien, to the 21st Century.

EVERYONE KNOWS THAT EXERCISE MAKES YOU STRONG, LIVING A healthy lifestyle helps you live longer and better, and curbing unnecessary expenses helps prepare for retirement. There is no shortage of books or articles that show you the list of positive goals to meet, but many people *fail* in fulfilling these.

Most people believe that they are born with either weak or strong willpower. They suffer from surrendering their lives to their self-imposed limitation. They believe that the weak will never create good habits, and the strong will always succeed at creating ones. So, if they fail their New Year's goals, they deem their innate willpower is poor and will not try to pursue their dreams.

In this chapter, we will cover what willpower is, discuss how it is depleted, and debunk the myth of what most people believe about it.

Science of Willpower

Willpower is the currency of the maximum amount of tasks that you can do in a given time. Although it sounds like it, it is not an unlimited source of inner energy that you can call upon at will to accomplish any tasks.

Every time you perform a task, you draw upon your willpower. Making a business decision, reading sad news, choosing the clothes to wear, selecting a movie to watch, and withholding your anger draw upon your willpower. Even trifling tasks draw upon your willpower. In hindsight, you need willpower to do everything that you want and need to do.

Willpower is one of the personal traits that defines positive outcomes in life, aside from intelligence. It is a better predictor of success than IQ score is. Psychologists have conducted many studies, and the result is consistent that people who possess good self-control or willpower are happier.[1] They maintain the following attributes:

- Better health
- Better weight
- High-salary job
- Better relationships

On the other hand, people with weak self-control show the following characteristics:

- High tendency to commit criminal activity
- Poorer
- Sicker
- Poorer relationships

Fortunately, willpower is something that you can learn to optimize. Therefore, everyone has a chance to succeed even without a first-class IQ score.

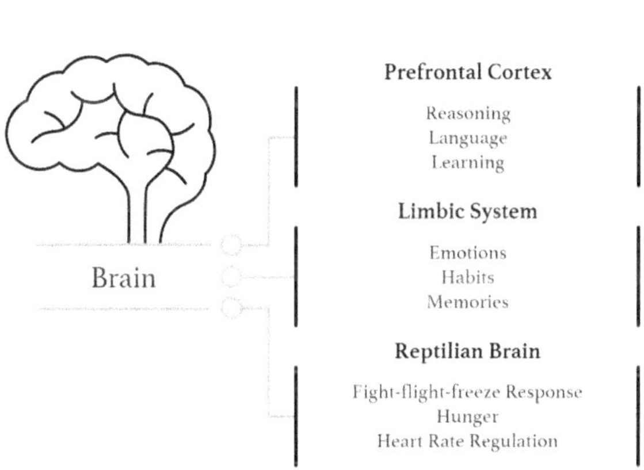

Simplified Brain Anatomy

FOR EASE OF UNDERSTANDING, allow me to simplify the brain's anatomy and categorize the brain's parts into two groups. We will call the first one ***primitive brain***, which consists of the limbic system and reptilian brain. The primitive brain ensured people's survival physically and socially during the Palaeolithic time (Stone Age). It triggers your response to fight, flight, freeze, reproduce, earn high social status, gain social acceptance, and seek reward.

- It pushes you to eat food at sight, particularly fat in case of hunting failure or famine.
- It wants you to mate to procreate in case you die of a disease picked up on your way to hunt.
- It compels you to enjoy all the sweetness in life in case of a natural disaster that could wipe you out.

At the outset, it favors instant gratification, with the simple reason that you may not live to see another day because of the fallen giant rock, or the next predator encounter. This brain played an important rule for our ancestors' survival.

Now, bring this primordial brain to our modern world and it will encourage you to eat that fast food, sweet donut, or pineapple tart to anticipate famine. It wants you to cheat on your spouse to mate with another person in case you die from wolf attacks. It wants you to enjoy modern entertainment while you still can before the next meteorite hits the earth.

The same primitive brain that our ancestors owned, we own it too. It still functions the same way as it did a million years ago. It prefers anything that could give you instant pleasure.

The good thing is, nature has given us another part of the brain that can help us analyze and perform higher-level thinking. This part of the brain is called the *prefrontal cortex*. It comprises over 10% of the total brain size. This brain part is responsible for self-control, decision-making, cognitive function, reasoning, problem-solving, interpreting good and bad things, and favoring a future bigger reward over instant gratification. The prefrontal cortex is the only thing that can stop our primitive brain from running amok in this modern world.

- It reminds you that there is an abundance of food and no need to binge eat.
- It reminds you that you will hurt your spouse if you mate with another person.
- It reminds you that you will not fulfill your goal if you don't quit playing video games and finish your assignment.

Without a strong prefrontal cortex, your primitive brain takes over, and your brain always defaults to choices that are easy and seem good despite the bad future impact they may cause. People with a poor prefrontal cortex exhibit impulsive behaviors and a diminished ability to solve problems.

Our prefrontal cortex grew bigger along with the brain after every evolution—from *Paranthropus robustus* to *Jomo habilis* to *Homo erectus* to *Jomo neanderthalensis* to us, modern humans, *Homo sapiens*. It is possibly an adaptation to handle the ever-increasing complexity of human life and the temptations each newer generation produces.

The prefrontal cortex helps us to be logical, so we don't wholly rely on the dominant primordial instinct of the primitive brain, which does not always work well in the modern world.

- Whenever you are challenged with temptation, the prefrontal cortex stops you to think of its impact before you give in to the temptation.
- Whenever you are given choices, the prefrontal cortex gives you the ability to make a good decision.
- Whenever you are confronted with annoyance, the prefrontal cortex nudges you to hold your anger.

The strength of your willpower depends on the strength of your prefrontal cortex, and it is exhaustible. When you exhaust it, your primitive brain gains control.

Psychologist Roy Baumeister and his colleagues conducted several experiments to prove that willpower is exhaustible. One of the experiments was a sampling test by sixty-seven students.[2] The experimenters requested these students not eat anything for at least three hours. The experimenters prepared chocolate cookies and radishes for their test. In the laboratory where the students were present, the experimenters baked the chocolate cookies to fill the room with cookie aroma. They assigned a group of students to eat at least two cookies, and the other group to eat at least two radishes. They only had five minutes to taste the assigned food. The experimenters observed that the group who ate radishes looked longingly to eat the chocolate cookies—trying hard to resist the temptation. After the tasting session, the experimenters crafted an impossible problem for these students to solve, and then left the room.

The students had thirty minutes to solve the problem, and could ring the bell if they gave up. The result was astonishing. All the students who ate radishes gave up earlier than the students who ate chocolate cookies. At the end of the sessions, the students who needed to eat the radishes admitted that they had forced themselves to eat radishes, and faced difficulty in resisting the chocolate cookies. The experiments showed that those who had exerted the willpower to resist the chocolate cookies had not much willpower left to do a problem-solving task. This experiment, along with many others, proved that willpower is exhaustible.

Why Self-Control Is Hard

Equipped with a logical brain, the adult human is smart enough to prefer a long-term big reward over a short-term small reward. Given two options—a brownie now or a healthy body later—one undoubtedly chooses the latter. But why do we still opt for the short-term small reward that has long-term consequences from time to time?

Consider the following scenario.

You are famished and your spouse brings home a large pack of your favorite brownies to indulge in together for your birthday celebration. Suddenly, it becomes increasingly appealing to eat it because you now view the reward is within grasp and obtainable at any moment. You drain a lot of self-control to spurn this offer.

> **Problem #1:** When the short-term reward is *present and available,* your perceived value of the short-term reward

becomes bigger, while the long-term reward becomes too distant.

Now, your spouse told you that if you don't eat the brownies, she will have to throw most of them away because she can't eat them all by herself and they won't last long. Dang! The punishment of wasting the money for the purchase is now attached to not eating it. The short-term reward is now seen as not only *more valuable,* but also *more likely to vanish.* It takes considerable effort to even consider your long-term bigger reward. You now need even higher self-control to treat this as a sunk cost and stick to your resolve.

Problem #2: People *prefer avoiding losses* to gaining something. Economists call this behavior loss aversion.

While you were still considering them, you stared at the enticing brownies cover, and within seconds your hand was already holding the brownies and your mouth was salivating.

Problem #3: Companies design the product and environment to lure you at a subconscious level.

The above problems exemplify most of the temptations we are facing today. It makes no economic sense, but that's our brain at work.

Willpower Crisis

Generation X and beyond are facing a *willpower crisis.* The unflinching temptations post-industrial age, combined with the technology in flux, are prodigious, and they are still adding up. The attention-grabbing advertisements, endless supply of entertaining videos, dopamine-driven social media's "like" counters, cheap fast food, unlimited TV shows, etc., have given a lot of challenges to our prefrontal cortex to *survive*.

Note: Dopamine is a feel-good neurotransmitter that your brain releases when you experience pleasure, such as achieving your goal. Anticipating rewards also releases dopamine.

Some restaurants install an artificial food aroma delivery system to deceive your sense of smell and tempt you to break your diet. Marketers style unhealthy food to look aesthetically pretty to increase its perceived healthiness. Companies use a limited-time sale to increase a false sense of urgency. Gadget manufacturers release better features, better battery life, and better display product regularly. Your phone that had the best features available last year seems obsolete to you now, and you are challenged by the headlong impulse to purchase the best of the best.

One reason car seller companies employ svelte women to pose with the cars at auto shows is to exploit male customers' self-control:

- Your primitive cortex sees the beauties and wants you to engage in conversation with them, which increases your chance to pass on your gene.
- Your primitive cortex implants a visual in you that women love you with that car, which also increases your chance to pass on your gene.
- Your primitive cortex notices the social status increase

in owning a car. You imagine that having higher social status makes you more likable, which gives you a higher opportunity to survive.

At the same time, the companies increase the chance to close the deal by getting you to buy new cars even if you don't need them. These marketing ploys are designed to please your primitive cortex and deplete your prefrontal cortex energy to fight back. All for the purpose of business profit.

If you are not careful, you could be unintentionally feeding yourself or your children with instant gratification too, and sacrificing long-term goals. It has become an alarmingly common sight to see parents giving their children a smartphone to watch videos just to get them to eat their meals. When they take the phones away from the children, the children get upset and stop eating. The parents would have no choice but to give the phone back to the children to calm them down. Unbeknown to them, they have granted their kids excessive dopamine release—an effect that is very similar to consuming drugs. These kids become accustomed to instant gratification and impair their own impulse control at an early age.

What Depletes Willpower?

Any event that requires your prefrontal cortex to come to your rescue when your primitive brain is in action depletes your willpower. If you need to clean up your house, but you prefer to watch TV now, you deplete your willpower when you forgo watching TV.

There are three broad categories of action that draw your willpower or require your prefrontal cortex intervention:

1. Resisting Temptation

When you resist any temptation, you drain your willpower. The greater the enticement, the more willpower you need to use.

Examples:

- Resisting the temptation to eat when you are watching a food review video.
- Managing your urge not to smoke when your close friend smokes during the lunch break.
- Preventing your laughter in public when you thought of something funny.
- Refusing the urge to look at the cat photo on your web browser when you are working on your thesis.
- Controlling your anger when you are losing your temper.
- Holding your tears when you are watching a sad Korean drama.
- Resisting the push to splurge on the branded clothing item that is on sale.

Crash diets never work for long because you dry up your willpower faster than it can be replenished. You are resisting too many temptations at a time. When you lose the battle, you give in and engorge more food, gaining more weight than when you started.

2. Making a Decision

This includes solving easy and difficult problems. You want to direct your willpower use for positive decision-making tasks and remove the unnecessary ones. The more complex the decision is, the more you need willpower. When you carry out the decision-making process with no effort, or run it without thinking (in an auto-pilot mode), you use very little to no willpower.

Decisions include:

- Making a decision at work
- Deciding which clothes to wear
- Comparing products before purchasing
- Planning the itinerary for your vacation
- Solving an algebra problem

When you have depleted a lot of willpower to make any further decision, your brain will conserve the remaining willpower and it will default to choosing the easiest option for you, and that includes not deciding at all, or settling for the recommended choice, even if it is not always the best choice for you.

In the case of high-profile leaders' extramarital affairs, are these people just dissatisfied with their life? Probably. But we should not dismiss the possibility that they had weakened their willpower. These are people who make many major decisions daily and have exhausted their willpower juice at the end of the day. Instead of laughing at these people, we should realize that the same regrettable, unsound mistakes could happen to us when we deplete our willpower.

3. Delaying Gratification

When you sacrifice your current comfort for a future goal, you draw upon your willpower. The more uncomfortable it is to do, the more willpower you draw.

These include:

- Dragging yourself to gym
- Eating that dreadful bowl of oatmeal
- Learning new Spanish vocabularies

Many New Year's resolutions fail because people are too optimistic about their goals. They add too many new routines to their lives, and spin their wheels. They suck up all their willpower in the pursuit of fulfilling all their new routines, but end up failing all of them. It would work if they were more strategical with their willpower use.

Depletion Limit

If you have allocated time to complete a few tasks based on the amount of willpower that you assess to be usable in a day, it should make no difference if you complete the tasks in any order, right? It makes a difference because you compromise the quality of the tasks you do later than earlier.

Our brain has a mechanism to put a halt on willpower use to prevent it from hitting rock bottom. This is beneficial from an evolution point of view: You need to reserve some amount of willpower in the system for an emergency—to help you devise last-minute decision-making for the best route escaping from packs of wolves, or to run away from a burning forest. It's a lot like losing body fat: Once you burn a lot of fat in the body, losing more fat becomes progressively difficult. Your body will prevent as much fat burning as possible to conserve for famine.

Suppose you plan to do the following:

- Learn music
- Complete a thesis
- Plan for your vacation
- Learn a new language

After learning music, you feel exhausted and are reluctant to do your thesis. Resuming your thesis feels heavy and intimidating for you. You have a higher urge to abandon it. Planning for your vacation feels more appealing to you to do next. If, however, you force yourself to complete your thesis, you will end up compromising the quality of that task. You can still complete the thesis, but it may contain more errors or be not as good compared to doing it with enough willpower.

As you can see, when you plan for a few complex tasks, the order of which you do first matters. If you exhaust your willpower on earlier tasks, you compromise the quality of your later tasks. Always favor completing the more important task first before completing the less important ones.

The same applies at the workplace too. When your job requires you to work long hours, you will exhaust all of your disposable willpower before you finish all your tasks. Thus, the tasks you complete last are the ones prone to errors. This highlights the revelation that long working hours do not equate to high productivity, as many people assume.

If you often get angry after work, never succeed at your diet, and procrastinate most of the time, the mainstream advice given is to:

- Take an anger management course
- Try harder
- Stay positive

Optimizing your willpower usage before anything else will be a sound strategy. In order to maximize your willpower usage for the best productivity, you need to:

1. Reduce your willpower consumption, so you can use it for a better purpose.
2. Replenish your willpower, so you can refill your willpower strategically.
3. Increase your willpower reserve, so you can manage an even greater challenge.

GETTING MOTIVATED to start a New Year's resolution is a good start, even though the battle is just the beginning. The real problem is executing and maintaining it for life. To do that, you need to carefully use your willpower, and not just wholly rely on it.

We are going to tackle the modern willpower challenge with a two-pronged approach: strengthen our willpower (internal), and handle environmental influence (external). Let's begin with the methods to ***reduce the willpower usage*** in the next chapter.

2

REDUCE WILLPOWER CONSUMPTION

 Sometimes you get the best light from burning a bridge.

— DON HENLEY

THERE ARE MANY SMALL WILLPOWER EXPENDITURES THAT YOU MAY be spending *daily* on unimportant matters. At a glance, you may think they are too minor of an issue for you to bother with, but you still employ your willpower for them. As a result, you complete each day with less usable willpower. The willpower wastage can rapidly pile up within a day for some people, and they exhaust their willpower before using it for any significant purpose.

You don't want to waste your willpower on something worthless in your life. Reducing your willpower consumption from these trivial matters allows you to reserve more willpower for later use. We will work on strategies to reduce willpower consumption.

Resisting Temptation

If you can avoid facing any temptation, you don't need to spend any willpower at all to resist them. Avoiding temptations may sound simple, and you may think that your willpower can handle all the teeming little temptations. However, most people tend to overestimate their willpower strength, called *restraint bias*. Their level of confidence is further inflated if they have succeeded in other areas of their lives. Having this mindset can be jeopardizing because of the overexposure to temptations and the neglect of mini temptations' accumulation that show up at any moment throughout the day. Before you realize it, all these temptations add up and drain your willpower. Research also shows that people who overestimate their willpower strength are often the ones who fail the willpower challenge.[1] Smokers who believe that they have strong willpower to quit smoking end up relapsing.

DISCARD TEMPTATION

LET'S begin by discarding temptations. An average person spends about four hours every day just resisting desires. The number of assailants from your environment is overwhelming. Marshaling your willpower resources to head-spear them is a suicide mission. We are dealing with scientists who can engineer food items that hook you with one bite, or the big supermarket chain that cleverly designs the floor plan and shelf layout with the goal of keeping you in the store longer, or music researchers who know which music to play to influence consumers' behavior, or wily experts who have a political proclivity to use polling locations to sway your vote. People who vote in church are more likely to vote for a conservative candidate.[2] These obscured environmental triggers could crush the goal of the unwary victims. Learning to notice them coming is crucial to handling them.

You use your willpower if the temptation is present and within your sight. To reduce the chances of resisting temptation, you need to *remove* the source of the temptation itself, or *restrict* your access to the temptation if you cannot remove the source. The proverb "out of sight, out of mind" has its wisdom. Start by identifying the things or situations that tempt you and then discard them.

Set up your home to support your goals. If you are trying to lose weight, don't stock up on potato chips in your kitchen cabinet. That alluring bag of chips will seduce you every time you open your cabinet to grab the oatmeal. Dispose of them to eliminate any temptation. Having a TV set with a video game console in your study room leaves you vacillating between studying and playing. Make everything that you are trying to avoid difficult to access.

When you are working, if you know that you are prone to browsing websites or reading unrelated emails, disconnect your Internet. Doing so draws upon your willpower as you need to resist the temptation to browse. If you must use the Internet for your work, install a software that tracks your computer time usage. It helps to identify the websites that often steal your attention when you are working, then blocks those websites during your productive hours.

If you often stop to check on the notifications on your phone, mute the notifications during your productive hours. Set up the push notification only on applications that are vital for you. Each pop-up notification demands your attention, whether you choose to ignore it or read it. Having many notifications you need to attend to contributes to your overall willpower consumption throughout the day.

Social media is another major factor that challenges your temptations.[3] When someone alludes to your post, or your picture in social media, the resistance is too strong for you to ignore. Its presence in your phone means it's available to interrupt you 24/7. If you are active in social media, you are draining a significant amount of your willpower just for this alone. It's a sad reality that the technology is a double-edged sword; it not only helps you to connect with people comfortably but also sucks your time and attention more than the person sitting next to you. You can constrain your social media by *restricting* its access only by computer. You may choose to delete your account to *remove* the temptation entirely if there is no good reason for you to use it.

If you are trying to control your spending, delete the shopping app on your phone, which unyieldingly prompts the flash deals, and unsubscribe yourself from the shopping mailing lists that send irresistible promotions every now and then. By receiving no marketing notices, you're lessening the urge to buy things that you don't need.

If you always pass by your favorite fast-food restaurant on your way home and are tempted to go there for dinner, use an alternate route if you have the choice. Help your brain gradually stop associating *the location* with *eating fast food* that it has learned over a long time.

If you have a problem with gambling, you should completely stay away from the casino. Casino designers design the idyllic environment to trap you subconsciously. The system uses coins to play because the experts know that parting with your dollars feels more painful than parting with your coins. They carefully choose the background music of every zone to attract gamblers. The bustling *ka-ching* sound in the slot machines influences you to think that you too can win some money. They design the carpet pattern to subtly contrive an exciting atmosphere. Free food is served to keep you there longer. If you are a gambling addict, even if you just go into the casino to check it out with no intention to play, your willpower is already assaulted by all these well-designed stimuli.

There are countless other scenarios, but you've got the idea. Make your access to bad habits as restricted as possible, and your access to good habits as convenient as possible. When you take the path of least resistance to perform good habits, you reduce your willpower usage.

SOCIAL CIRCLE

Your social circle influences your willpower in two ways:

1. They become your normalcy

PEOPLE HAVE a penchant to mirror the habits of those they spend the most time with. Psychologists call this the *Social Proximity Effect*, or the tendency to fit in with others or attempt to act like them to be accepted socially. If your roommate always wakes up late, you are likely going to wake up late too. You compare your standard against people around you. Everyone is doing it, and so should you. You don't want others to see you as an outlier. Their *normal* becomes your *normal*. A study shows that individuals who spend time with drinkers are more likely to form a habit of drinking.[4]

2. They can contradict with your goals

Spending time with friends or family who conflict with your goals reduces the opportunity of success:

- You face the temptation from your spouse to watch a TV series, when it is time for you to study for your exam.
- Your old craving reignites when watching your roommate playing video games while you are trying to finish your assignment.
- You find it hard to reject the invitation from your friends to go clubbing, when it is a chance for you to go to the gym.

Maybe you don't think it is significant, because you believe you can just ignore them. It is harder than you think when all of your social circle contradicts your plan. Imagine how much willpower you need to spare to face the accumulated temptations every day: from the morning burger that your spouse enjoys for breakfast, to the French fries your coworker eats for lunch, to the cheesy pizza your spouse has for dinner.

After using your willpower for your own activities, the temptations generated by your social circle become highly irresistible, and willpower failure soon ensues. Dieters who spend most of the time with non-dieters often fail. Sociologists estimated that the risk of a person to become obese is 57% if he or she has a friend who becomes obese.[5] This is a waste of willpower usage, because you are not spending your willpower on really productive activities.

The good thing is, the reverse applies. If you are spending time with people who are health conscious, exercise junkies, and non-smokers, you will feel guilty to eat bad, be lazy, or smoke—and draw upon your willpower. You are very inclined to do the same as what the surrounding people do. For this to work in your favor, you must espouse the same behaviors as the people in your social circle.

When you are trying to quit smoking, you will see better results if you immerse yourself in a community of individuals who are also trying to quit smoking. A study published in *Nicotine &* *Tobacco Research* shows that an online community can help improve the adherence to smoking cessation.[6] You get the support of like-minded individuals when you are hitting setbacks. You feel ashamed when you can't abide by your decision in the group to quit smoking.

The same applies to enrolling in an online weight-loss community. A study published in 2015 showed that being connected in a network of other people who are trying to lose weight results in an increased chance of weight-loss success, compared to those who don't.[7]

As you use your willpower positively, everything that you do leans toward the success of your goal.

- The support from the group lightens your burden to deal with setbacks alone, which helps to *reduce* your willpower consumption.
- The peer pressure *draws* upon your willpower if you don't keep up with what you have committed to the group.

Whom you spend your time most with defines who you are. Ideally, you need to spend more time with people who share the same goal, and distance yourself from people who encourage your bad habits. If you are a parent of young children, recognize that your children will likely grow up following your behaviors.[8] Obese parents will likely raise obese children. Smoker parents will likely raise smoker children. Build some good habits as a role model for your descendants, if not for yourself.

ILLNESS

WHEN YOU ARE DEALING with a chronic illness or injury that debilitates you, you continuously draw upon your willpower to withstand the suffering. You need to endure the pain and resist the temptation not to scream or cry out in pain.

This is the reason convalescents sleep a lot, because their immune system needs to conserve enough energy to fight off the illness. There is not much spare energy for decision-making, or building good habits. If the illness is something that you can treat soon, have it done as soon as possible, to avoid the continuous waste of willpower. However, if it is not something that you can cure immediately, be mindful of your willpower usage on other activities. You are already living day by day with less willpower.

If you have the luxury of time for a non-emergency treatment that you predict will cause lingering pain, plan to do it strategically.

- If the treatment will cause a few hours of pain (e.g., tooth extraction), do it during non-working hours or on a day when you have fewer tasks to do to minimize the impact of the depleted willpower on the quality of your work.
- If the treatment will lead to discomfort for months or years (e.g., surgery, applying dental braces), be wary of introducing any new habit or any action that requires a lot of willpower as you weaken your willpower to the anguish.

TERRIFYING NEWS

Reading or watching news drains your willpower. Some people emotionally binge-eat after watching saddening news on TV. Terrifying news depicts probable death. We tend to think that we will live for a long time. We don't like others to remind us of our own mortality and feel terrified when someone does it to us. Our impulse to enjoy everything amplifies after we rediscover that death is inevitable. Psychologists called this phenomenon *mortality salience*.

You may have noticed the scary warning images some countries have emblazoned on their cigarette packs. They are intended to discourage smokers from smoking and to break the habit by reminding them of their mortality. However, it does not always work. The thought of the grotesque image that could happen to yourself weakens willpower. Some smokers perceive that as a threat to challenge or take away their freedom, which further provokes their compulsive desire to smoke. If you just had a stressful day and are trying to quit smoking, this scary image adds a burden to your willpower to further make you lose self-control. The force of your primitive brain becomes stronger and convinces you that smoking will make you feel better.

When the United Kingdom first introduced the grotesque image on the cigarette package in 2001, there was no significant drop in the number of smokers.[9] In fact, the count remained stable for the next four years. It was well-intentioned, but didn't yield the expected result. [10]

You can observe a similar situation from viewing awful news. Watching any terrifying scene causes you to picture yourself in the event, and analyze some possibilities of what you could do to prevent it, or to save yourself from the tragedy. You think about the possibility of it happening to your close family members too. All these induce fear in your mind and weaken your willpower. That is why fear sells better.

It is no wonder that many people give in to the advertisement temptation presented during the terrifying news. A study showed that people rate high-status items more favorably after watching depressing news.[11] Our primitive brains convince us that prestigious items inflate social status, and it is important for our survival. Marketing experts know this and try to amplify the advertisements' effect with terror.

One example is the terror during the 9/11 tragedy.[12] The extreme fear terrified people; however, in the aftermath, the purchase of goods increased. People started to buy luxury items, such as cars, in high quantity during that period. Shouldn't people have been more careful with their spending because the global crisis was impending? This is the same reason as when you are overly consumed by terror. It becomes easier for you to give in to any temptation that makes you feel good, such as buying things.

If there is nothing that you can do after watching terrifying news, you might as well not watch it to weaken your willpower. Most of us can't do anything about it, anyway. We obviously can't avoid terrifying/saddening news altogether. Such bad news is everywhere: in your friend's Facebook posts, Instagram posts, national TV, newspaper. Unless your career requires you to keep pace with the news, avoid it as much as possible. You may think that you will miss out on any important information. Yes, you will be slower to get the news compared to people who read news, but I assure you that you won't be the last person on earth to hear bad news, unless you have no social interaction. News as important as the COVID-19 virus outbreak will still reach your ears through word of mouth, or your friends, or your HR department sending out preventive measures emails. You can then deliberately obtain the news if you wish to know more.

Think about it. How much of the news that you watch contains information that matters to you? Perhaps only a very small amount of it. The majority of it covers:

1. Natural disasters, which increase your anxiety.
2. War or crime, which instills fear.
3. Public figure gossip, which encourages you to gossip.
4. Politics, which causes agitation and stimulates you to argue with those who oppose your opinion.

Imagine how much you can free up from your mind, and how much time you'll save, to do things you love.

Making Decisions

There are many tasks you do every day. Some of them do not need you to decide anything, because they are run on auto-pilot in your brain. You don't need to remember to brush your teeth before bed, or to take a shower after returning home from work. These kinds of tasks do not drain willpower. On the other hand, you also do many things that require a decision-making process. Such tasks drain your willpower, even if they are just trivial decisions.

This becomes significant if you need to use your willpower for unnecessary decisions repeatedly every day. For example:

- Deciding what clothes to wear (except if you are a fashion celebrity)
- Remembering if you have paid your tuition fee
- Remembering if you have taken your medicines or vitamins

All this minor decision making adds up and reduces your total disposable willpower of the day. Learning to trim unnecessary decision making is essential to conserve your overall willpower. This could extend to life-saving benefits. If you are a surgeon and have an upcoming major operation appointment, protecting yourself from decision fatigue beforehand allows you to make better decisions during the operation.

REPEATED TASKS

YOU NEED to keep things systematic to simplify your decision-making process and reduce your willpower usage of repeated tasks to the minimum.

Set up an SOP, Standard Operating Procedure, to determine a fixed list of clothes you will wear from Monday to Sunday or, better yet, wear the same clothes every day if it is viable for you.

This way, you don't tap into your willpower daily just to decide which clothes to wear.

Set up GIRO payments for all of your bills so you don't need to keep tracking your bills' payment due dates.

Pre-define your workout schedule, so you don't need to remember when is the right time to work out.

If you cook, write down all the foods that you like and spread the menu over the course of a week. This way, you know what ingredients you need to purchase and what to cook for an entire week. You also minimize the trips to buy groceries every time you decide to cook a certain food that you don't have the ingredients for.

Home is the place most of us spend a lot of time at. Determine what you do or require most at home and automate them if you can. Home automation can be costly and time-consuming to set up. If you have the budget, you could do many things to automate your routine, such as auto-turn on the white noise machine when you go to bed at night, or auto-light the house when you reach home, to conserve some willpower.

Tidying up your house can help you find things efficiently and occupy less space in your memory to recall the placement of things you need to use daily. It indeed takes a lot of time to do that, but it is worth the effort to reduce the willpower waste for all the household members. Read *The Art of Tidying Up* by Marie Kondo to overhaul your house clutter.

If you always find it difficult to remember which switch is for which light at home, put stickers on your switches so you won't need to run much cognitive function when you return from work with already-depleted willpower.

If you always have trouble finding the correct charging cable out of multiple cables for your phone, spending time organizing your cables will save your willpower juice in the future.

The phone is one of the most used items in our daily lives. You can organize your apps so that the most-used ones are all together and on the first screen to minimize the number of times you need to swap your phone's screen. Spend some time tinkering with an automation app; it can come in handy to help you automate many things that you repeatedly require your phone to do, which will save you a lot of willpower juice.

The list that you have may vary. You may be lucky to have a helper, or a virtual assistant who can help you handle your food, bills payment, or house chores; in that case, you can look into other areas of your life that need to be systematized.

Unfinished Tasks

The solution to plan for unfinished tasks may sound simple, but not many people practice that. Let's get into the reason why it is effective. When you have piles of emails to reply to, documents to attend to, letters to follow up with, or other matters to get back to, you sometimes find yourself frozen with these overwhelming tasks, even though you know that you can just clear them off one after another and every plate will soon be off the table. But you are often not motivated to do it. The thought of much unfinished business fills up your brain and stops you from taking any action. Just looking at your desk with the muddles of letters and documents stifles action. The old matters are left unattended, while you introduce more new tasks and increase the backlog even more.

When you move on with your life—say, while you're at a movie theatre—your mind will sometimes mire in these unfinished tasks. When you are eating your dinner, you get the nudge from your mind again. It goes on to your bed, and you may find it difficult to fall asleep. Imagine how much willpower you are wasting fretting over this. You are losing willpower daily just to unfreeze your mind in order to move on with your tasks. This is another possible hidden waste of willpower in your daily life.

To fix this, you need to establish a plan to clear all these tasks soon, not later, so you will stop wasting your willpower resource daily. Research supports the evidence that unfulfilled tasks persist in your mind until you make a plan for it.[13] You have tons of tasks on hand, both in personal and professional life. You need to create a plan to complete each of them. You do not have to clear the tasks soon, but you must have a plan on when to do them. You must not fool yourself by saying that you will clear all your letters next month when you know you will not do it. Your subconscious mind knows it.

Start looking at all your unfulfilled items and make a specific plan regarding when to complete them. You can use a list to maintain all your tasks with their specific due date, and you know you can rely on this master list to check if there is anything important to clear every day. You shall keep this master list as simple and easy to manage as possible.

Introducing too many unnecessary elements makes maintaining this list a chore and takes more time.

Cross the tasks that require only a minute to settle off your to-do list immediately. When you finish clearing up your letters, you may realize that perhaps only 50% of them require your attention. The documents that have been in your "in" trays for months may be mostly items for reference. This allows you to take a heavy load off your shoulders.

Planning for your tasks' completion saves you a lot of willpower consumption and allows you more opportunity to expand it for other purposes. Obviously, the best way is to prevent your tasks from piling up in the first place. We all know sometimes life gets in the way; however, as soon as you have the chance, start making a plan for them, and reduce the hidden waste of your willpower.

The same applies to remembering temporary information, such as:

- Trying to remember to pay bills later.
- Trying to remember to call your parents later.
- Trying to remember to buy an extra pair of socks when you go to a supermarket later.
- Trying to remember to fix the light bulb later.

Free up your memory by jotting down all these tasks whenever possible. Attempting to remember many things taxes your willpower.

CHOICE OVERLOAD

IF YOU WISH to exhaust someone's willpower, present them with multiple options to decide. This is especially true for perfectionists or people of high status. They know that choosing one option means forfeiting the rest of the options. They want to be sure they choose the best of the best. This activity depletes their willpower.

Consider the famous jam experiment that psychologists conducted in a supermarket in 2000.[14] At one time, the supermarket placed 24 choices of jam on the shelves, and another time it placed six choices thereof. The result was that only 4% of the individuals who stopped by purchased the jam of 24 choices, whereas an astounding 31% of people who stopped by purchased the jam of six choices. Buyers were overwhelmed by the superfluous choices, and decided not to decide at all.

Shopping is supposed to be an enjoyable experience, and you wouldn't think that it would exhaust a lot of your willpower. Shopping fatigues your willpower more than you realize it does. With the plethora of choices available in the market today, you will soon be bogged down to:

- Choose one brand of clothes over another.
- Determine the best toy gift from over 200 choices for your friend's child.
- Select the bubble tea you want to drink, level of sugar, and the size.
- Decide the coffee you want to order, type of creamer,

amount of creamer splash, and type of sweetener.
- Choose a swanky pair of shoes for your friend's wedding.

Other experiences in the shopping mall:

- Eluding the marketer who rushes to you when you were walking to the restroom.
- Lining up to buy your favorite food.
- Maintaining your poise when you run into a shopper who has just cut in front of you in line.
- Resisting the temptation of the sweet-smelling chocolate cookies that you have banned yourself from eating.
- Selecting one out of twenty photos you took to post on your Instagram page.

These are also the reasons some people who come back from vacation feel more mentally exhausted than before vacation.

There is no escape from the ever-growing list of choices available in the market today. It is patently clear that you fatigue your willpower with multiple options. Understanding that making a choice is a willpower-consuming act can help you plan your tasks wisely.

Often, if you can let go of your perfectionist behavior, you can keep your choices to the minimum if the decision is not that important. You don't need to get all other features that you know you will lose for forgoing other options, as long as you are clear of the necessary features you need. For example, there are many websites that recommend electronics, gadgets, or other items. If you read a few recommendations and you know what features are the absolute requirements for you, then you are set because no matter what option you choose, you ought to miss out on some features the alternative has.

Doing so not only saves you time but also reduces your willpower use on unimportant selections. Think about the time and effort you need to spend by voluntarily submerging yourself into a multitude of choices if what you need to decide is not all that important. Besides, too much choice leaves you feeling more dissatisfied and unhappy with your purchase.

ADAPTATION TO A NEW ENVIRONMENT

WHEN YOU ENTER AN UNFAMILIAR ENVIRONMENT, you unconsciously use a lot of willpower to conform to the new surroundings. Your brain associates a new environment with uncertainty and laden with potential threats. When our ancestors scouted a new territory, they needed to be extra vigilant. The sound of a water drop could indicate nearby perilous predators. Footprints on the trail suggested there were existing inhabitants who could be a threat.

During your travels to an unfamiliar country, everything seems new to you and your brain naturally puts you on guard. You have a bunch of things you need to watch out for:

- Is this stranger who is asking me for directions trustworthy?
- Is there a camera watching me?

- Will I offend the passerby if I ask this question?
- Is my wallet still in my pocket?

Similarly, when you just join a new company, you tend to use a lot of willpower to adapt:

- Can I trust this coworker?
- Is this the work my superior expects?
- Am I accepted by my peers?

The effect amplifies when the people around you are in a foul mood, because it gives you a sign that something unpleasant is going on and you must increase your vigilance. Now, this is not something you can always choose to reduce; sometimes circumstances require you to move to an unfamiliar environment. It also does not mean that you should avoid entering a new environment; in fact, stimulating your brain with a new environment flourishes your brain cells. At least, be aware that this action saps your willpower, so you can plan your willpower usage ahead of time.

Delaying Gratification

Researchers linked the ability to delay gratification to future success. It goes without saying, the result is apparent because:

- When you delay gratification to play a video game, you spend more time doing your homework.
- When you delay gratification to eat fast food, you end up eating a hearty home-cooked meal.

- When you delay gratification to watch a TV series, you resort to spending time with your family.

All the outcomes lead to better odds of success. Delaying gratification is hard, and you need a good amount of willpower to achieve success. Let's see next what you can work on to help you reduce the willpower consumption when you delay gratification.

PERSONAL MOTIVATION

PERSONAL MOTIVATION IS A DRIVING force to do anything you must do. When you have a strong intrinsic motivation, you are less likely to shirk your responsibilities and use less willpower to combat procrastination. A scientific study at the University of Albany suggests that people with internal goals and desires do not get their willpower depleted easily.[15] If you are saving money for your wedding, you are aiding your willpower to curb your spending, compared to when you don't have any self-commitment at all. If you are studying hard so you can teach your sister who cannot afford to go to school, you already have the upper hand to combat procrastination, compared to others who don't have any inherent reason to do what they do.

Certainly, it is easier said than done, and not everyone has a strong purpose for doing something. Most of the time the reason—if you have one—just is not solid enough to keep you motivated for long. You plan to stop eating donuts because of your obesity, but then you will just eat one today because you can always restart tomorrow.

Let's look at some techniques you can recruit to help you increase your motivation and lower your willpower consumption.

1. Learn to love what you do

The amount of willpower required to complete a task for one person is not the same as that of others. When you are working on tasks that you find enjoyable, you use less willpower. But if you don't enjoy doing the tasks, you need greater willpower.

People who drag their feet to the office to work on things they don't like and face their difficult coworkers consume a lot of willpower. They are mostly not self-motivated to do their best, and prone to making poor decisions. After work, they have trouble controlling their emotions at home because they have exhausted a lot of willpower at work.

People who truly love their jobs perform better at work. In a six-month experiment, University of Oxford's Saïd Business School showed a clear relationship between happy employees and high productivity.[16] Their willpower does not get sucked by dreaded tasks, a domineering boss, or backstabbing colleagues. These people have been using less willpower when working on the tasks they need to do. Therefore, they can conserve a lot of willpower, and channel its use for better decision-making and productivity. It also leaves them with enough willpower in reserve for self-control at home when they return from work.

The maxim "a happy employee equals a productive employee" is not far from the truth. Learn to love what you do. You get to experience high satisfaction in life if you are paid for doing things you love and are skillful at them, and your work benefits the world at the same time.

Surely, not many people have the luxury to have a career they love or choose what to do for a living. Others may be unlucky to have to deal with nasty coworkers or overbearing bosses, which you can't control much to make your work enjoyable. If so, and if your situation permits, quitting your job is the best course of action, allowing you to reinvest your resources on another job.

If you love your job, but it is sometimes boring or monotonous, you still have control to make it enjoyable.

- Maybe you can perform your tasks in a more challenging manner by changing the way you normally do them. For example, if you are a chef, you can switch to use your non-dominant hand to do your work.
- Maybe you can optimize your tasks by finding creative ways to speed up your pace. For example, if you are a programmer, you can build some scripts to automate some of your repeated tasks.
- Maybe you can increase the difficulty of your tasks to learn new things. For example, if you are an accountant, you can request to handle a more complex company account.

Whatever you do, you can try to upgrade yourself and learn new skills, and your job won't be that meaningless to you.

Apply the same approach to other areas of your life. If you are struggling to lose body fat, make your diet enjoyable too.

Setting up too many restrictions in your pursuit hampers your enjoyment and does not work well. It is human nature that the more you restrict yourself from doing something, the more you want to do it. Research showed that people who restrict their food during dieting bounce back with more weight gain, compared to when they didn't diet at all.[17] What you can learn from this finding is not to abandon any diet and eat all you want, but to recognize that you can do better with your diet by not constraining yourself too much. You can cut back on unhealthy food but allow yourself flexibility to still be able to eat your favorite food from time to time. When you enjoy the invigorating pleasure of a healthy lifestyle, you will voluntarily stop eating unhealthy food because you build the tendency to dislike the uncomfortable feeling caused by the unhealthy food.

2. Reverse the economy of your action

Remember the earlier story in which your spouse will throw away the large pack of your favorite brownies if you don't want to eat them? You become less motivated to fulfill your goal when there is a punishment to do it. The logical solution is to treat it as a sunk cost, and move on. Reflect upon the future higher cost of staying obese compared to the low cost of the brownies you are giving up now. But that is difficult for most of us to do, especially with money at stake and with the instant pleasure that brownies provide.

On the other hand, credit cards offer you reward points every time you splurge; you are discouraged to save. Restaurants offer you more points when you order more food; you can't resist ordering that extra ice cream just to get more points even if you are already full. In short, you are rewarded for enabling bad habits, and the force of everything around you contradicts your motivation.

To fix this, you can reverse the situation by self-imposing a punishment when you derail from your goal, and rewarding yourself when you stick to your commitment. For example, you can sign up on a website that allows you to put down some money and pay that money to other members if you do not stick to your pledge. Or, you can purchase a gym membership if you find yourself procrastinating when it comes to exercising. The thought of wasting the membership fee punishes you whenever you attempt to skip again. Research has shown that this principle is effective; the larger the money at stake, the higher the probability of succeeding.[18] I exhort that you only apply this method as your last resort if you still have a problem with commitment after applying the principles learned in this book. You shouldn't need to spend money for this if you can control your willpower well.

The same applies to rewarding yourself to reinforce positive behaviors. For each day you quit smoking, you can save the money to get a massage. Immediate reward works best. By doing this, you are recruiting more allies toward helping your willpower, instead of letting the default situations conspire against it. Be aware that using rewards to encourage positive behaviors does not work well for children. Incentivizing exemplary behavior can hamper children's motivation. The children begin to use the award as the anchor to their motivation, instead of building it intrinsically. When the reward is absent, so is their motivation.

3. Self-monitoring

You know that not controlling your diet will ruin your health in the future, but the future just seems so far away, and it is more enticing to just enjoy the present reward. It certainly won't cause any harm if you just begin your diet plan tomorrow, right? Alas, the human is a fallible creature. To overcome this short-sightedness, you must monitor your progress. Log your diet plan, your weight, your non-smoking streak, your alcohol-free days, your exercise habit, and anything that you wish to change. Research shows that smokers who self-monitor reduce their rate of smoking by 61%.[19]

Self-monitoring is tedious, and the hardest part to maintain. People would rather cut down their calories after being told that they have exceeded the quota for the day than log their food's calories. Most people give it up after monitoring for a while, even though it is an effective tool, because people usually underestimate the amount of alcohol they drink, the amount of sugar they consume, the amount of cigarettes they smoke, and other addictive activities. When you can see records that show how you have been doing, it becomes easier to convince yourself of what your future will hold. If you have not been following through on your commitment, it serves as an eye-opener for you. Looking at your weight trend that increases every week instantly warns you that you will be morbidly obese in the next two years if you don't change your lifestyle. Likewise, when you see you have been progressing, even at a slow pace and not outwardly noticeable, you know you've been doing well and feel motivated to continue your pursuit. You can stop logging when fulfilling your commitment becomes second nature.

HABIT

ANOTHER POWERFUL METHOD TO slash the amount of willpower use is setting up a habit. Successfully forming a habit reduces your willpower consumption a lot. It is not the habit that causes the lowered willpower consumption; it is the auto-pilot result thereof. You need an extensive amount of willpower to build a new habit, but once you have formed the habit, you will draw little to no willpower to execute the habit.

If you have been making your bed after waking up all your life, your brain runs on auto-pilot mode to get you to do that without needing any push from your willpower. Not making your bed, in turn, makes you feel strange, and that draws some willpower. Going for a jog after work used to cost you a lot of willpower, but when you turn the activity into your habit, it costs less or no willpower. You will eventually reach a point where, when you skip it, you will feel antsy and eager to get out and exercise.

The same applies to bad habits too. If you always eat potato chips while watching TV, your brain connotes snacking with watching, and makes it your default state. You will always want to snack every time you turn on a TV. This behavior is further reinforced every time you eat popcorn while watching in a cinema.

Once you form a habit, deviating from your habit drains your willpower:

- If you practice a good habit, you drain willpower when you veer from the good habit.
- If you practice a bad habit, you drain willpower when you veer from the bad habit.

Twenty-two days are too short for most people to form a new habit that sticks. Studies suggest that it takes on average sixty-six days to make the habit stick.[20] If you can consistently execute the task by sixty-six days, you have a higher chance to form the task into a habit. If you find yourself often forgetful to maintain the streak, using a task tracking app can be useful to remind you.

Continue to build new good habits after you successfully form one—one after another, not altogether, otherwise you risk draining too much energy from your willpower tank, and fail to create any habit at all.

Your habit defines you. Choose wisely. The result of your habit is not immediate, but stacking good ones that are most relevant to you can change your life in a year, five years, or a decade. In addition, the benefits of any good habit serve you exponentially because you get to unlock more opportunities in your life. If you have not taken charge of your life to build good habits for yourself, you are missing out on a lot of opportunities.

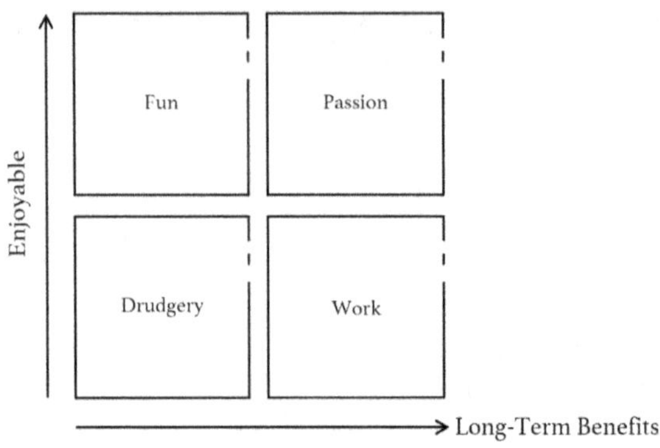

Types of Habits

Determine what your current habits are with the above matrix. To lead a more fulfilled life, you want to accumulate as many habits that are enjoyable and serve your long-term objective—passion. Most of the time, habits that benefit your long-term goal are not enjoyable—work—but you shall convert as many of them as possible into enjoyable habits to reduce your willpower consumption. Learn to enjoy them and hard work can become a labor of love. In contrast, habits that do not support your long-term goal are usually enjoyable—fun. You shall break these habits to channel your energy into forming ones that benefit your goals. Sometimes life forces you to do menial tasks that do not contribute to your long-term goals—drudgery. Whenever opportunity arises, you should quit these. Adjusting your willpower usage allows you to form new habits with ease and maintain them for life.

WE HAVE SEEN a lot of willpower waste in our lives, be it negligible or major waste. You may already waste it repeatedly on unimportant matters without your awareness. To gain the most out of this, you shall apply as many of these principles as possible because the vast number of external stimuli clearly outnumber you. Applying just a bit of these does not work, and will still make you prone to fall off the wagon. You have removed cigarettes and ashtrays from your home, but at break time you continue to join your colleagues who offer cigarettes to you.

Practically, it is not possible for you to reduce the willpower temptation to near zero. Not in this 21st century when big companies spend money to exploit your primitive brain. Temptations never cease. When you walk into a seemingly innocuous supermarket just to do your shopping, a promoter gives you a free sample of food to sell you food that you don't need but you probably want. Your primitive brain instinct awakens and tells you, "Take the food while it is free."

There are many other examples, but you get the idea. Predetermining a set of established behaviors oriented toward your goals increases the odds of succeeding.[21] While you can't eliminate all the willpower-sucking variables, understand that you have controls to reduce as many as you can, and relish the unbounded willpower reserve that you can redirect for creative use and a bigger purpose in life.

We will see in the next chapter how to *replenish willpower* so you can maintain sufficient reserve throughout the day.

3

———

REPLENISH WILLPOWER

> There is virtue in work and there is virtue in rest.
> Use both and overlook neither.
>
> — ALAN COHEN

WHEN YOU USE UP YOUR WILLPOWER FASTER THAN YOU CAN replenish it, you reach low willpower state, which leaves you prone to making grave decisions, or surrendering to temptations. This invariably happens when you are adopting too many new habits in one go or handling many demanding tasks. Let's look at some strategies to restock your willpower throughout the day and during emergencies, so you will be ready to face any willpower challenge at any time.

Glucose

The human brain is only about 2% the size of the total body weight, but it is the major consumer of glucose in the body. The brain consumes about 20% of energy derived from glucose or sugar. People with low blood sugar level (hypoglycemia) face the problem of low willpower, as do diabetic patients, because of the low glucose amount in their brains.[1] Evidence in 2011 showed propensity toward crime among people with diabetes.[2] Not that all hypoglycemia sufferers are bad people; they just need to be careful with their self-control. If mishandled, their lack of self-control could influence their behaviors and lead to criminal activities.

Note: Your body breaks down the carbohydrate food you consume into glucose, which is absorbed into your bloodstream. Your pancreas then releases insulin to shuttle the glucose into your body cells and brain. When the glucose is not immediately needed by your body to function, it is stored as glycogen in liver and muscles.

The court system acknowledges the problem with lack of glucose, and it was used as a legal defense in a court in 1991.[3] Alasdair Padmore was a type 1 diabetes patient. He killed his friend by stabbing him with a kitchen knife at around 9 p.m. after returning from a gym. His blood glucose reading before the murder was low, at less than 2.2 mmol/L; normal level is 7.8 mmol/L. At the trial, the judge ruled that he was suffering from hypoglycemia at the time of the murder, and thus acquitted. The judge did not consider him a murderer, but under the influence of hypoglycemia. Understandably, this outcome infuriated the public.

A STUDY of more than a thousand court decisions on parole hearings, to determine if inmates should be granted early prison release, found that the judges were lenient after breakfast and after lunch.[4] They were more likely to consider a prisoner's release after a meal. This likelihood decreased steadily over time after a meal. If you are the last prisoner to be heard before the judge took a lunch break, the judge is more likely to reject the early release. Deciding to release prisoners requires willpower to deal with the potential perilous problems of early release. Thus, it is easier to stick to the status quo or reject the early release.

The result suggested that the breakfast or lunch break replenished the glucose in the system that had been used up throughout the judging process. Was it really the glucose in the brain that fueled the willpower? A further study corrected the error of this analysis. It wasn't that the judges were harsher later after the break; it was that the prisoners without legal representation were scheduled for hearings at the end of each session before break, which explains the low chance of granting releases.[5]

In 2007, psychologists conducted another study that fit neatly with the original assumption to measure the self-control of participants who were already drained of their willpower.[6] They gave a glucose drink to a group of participants, and another drink with artificial sweetener to another group. The former group improved their self-control on subsequent tasks given, while the latter displayed low self-control. This study concluded that glucose restores the willpower energy.

The theory that ingesting sugar replenishes willpower sparked criticism. For one thing, exerting cognitive demanding effort does not reduce glucose in the brain.[7] If there is no glucose reduction when you use your willpower, then it makes no sense that ingesting glucose restocks your willpower.

Drinking glucose for the sake of replenishing willpower is ill-advised. Sugar is likely one of the things that you are aiming to cut down by training your willpower for, and yet you must ingest glucose to replenish your willpower to avoid sugar. Avoid consuming sugar as much as possible, lest your body develops insulin resistance. What about the conclusion in regard to the participants who drank a sugary drink performing better at a self-control task? This can be explained in the follow-up experiments.

Note: Insulin resistance is the condition when your body cells no longer respond well to the insulin produced by the pancreas. The glucose remains in the bloodstream for a longer time and not used in your brain. This excess glucose then gets stored as fat. Insulin resistance can lead to several problems such as diabetes, heart disease, and obesity. Excessive sugary food consumption and an unhealthy lifestyle are the primary cause of this.

In 2012, scientists attempted to replicate the glucose effect on willpower. They discovered that the effect on willpower replenishment comes from the presence of glucose in the mouth and not from the ingestion of it.[8] The scientists prepared two types of water solution—one containing glucose, and one containing artificial sweetener. They divided fifty-one students into two groups, with one group gargling the glucose solution and another one gargling the artificial sweetener solution. The former group did better with a self-control test afterward compared to the latter group. This finding suggested that when the sugar is gargled and touches our mouth, it binds the receptors in our mouth, which activates the reward system in the brain and gives you the motivation to do what you need to do.[9] They showed this method worked to remind you of your goals, briefly after swishing the sugar. We need further research to unveil its long-term effect on self-control.

I do not use the glucose gargling method myself because of its impracticality, but I have included the information in this book so you can avoid the blunder of drinking a sugary solution to increase willpower and mess with your diet. It is clear that hypoglycemia patients have reduced self-control, but that does not mean consuming sugar replenishes self-control in people with a normal blood sugar level. Correlation does not mean causation.

Rest

Rest, which includes nighttime sleep, naps, and relaxing, replenishes your willpower. There is no denying that good quality sleep is needed to stock up your willpower to full capacity. Your prefrontal cortex works well when it is well rested. Combine that with the state of your brain that is refreshed, first thing in the morning is the time of the day that makes you feel you can do almost everything you have planned for.

Students who do not sleep enough for the next day's exam operate with lowered willpower capacity aside from the feeling of sleepiness, which hampers the ability to solve complex problems. When you don't sleep well, you start the day with less willpower. It is no wonder many sleep-deprived people are prone to making poor decisions throughout the day because of their reduced brain capacity and low willpower reserve. You shall definitely invest your time in achieving a good night's sleep to maximize your willpower replenishment aside from the other numerous benefits it offers. I covered a detailed plan and strategy to achieve quality sleep in *Peak Human Clock*.

Taking a brief nap that is less than forty-five minutes replenishes some willpower too, albeit not as much as a solid full night's sleep. For the avoidance of doubt, **relaxing** does not mean browsing social media, which often results in increased anxiety. Modern society often confounds smartphone usage with relaxation. True relaxation refers to calming your nervous system and revitalizing your mind, such as getting a massage, walking in nature, or listening to music. Strategically taking a break to relax for willpower restoration is often overlooked, and regrettably many people judge it as a form of laziness.

Serotonin

Neurotransmitters are the messengers in your body that transmit messages from the nerve cells (neurons) to the cells throughout your body. They tell your brain to stabilize your mood, help you fall asleep, make you motivated, etc. An imbalance of neurotransmitters causes anxiety, depression, and other mood disorders. Healthy lifestyle, regular exercise, and good stress management can help to balance the function of neurotransmitters.

There are more than a hundred neurotransmitters in your body. Four of the famous ones are:

1. Dopamine

This is the brain reward system. Your brain releases dopamine when you succeed at your goal, achieve your lifelong dream, or something rewarding happens. The release makes you experience joy and pleasure. People often exploit the same feeling by playing video games, gambling, or taking drugs.

2. Serotonin

Serotonin regulates your mood and promotes the feeling of happiness. When you have a meager amount of serotonin, you experience a foul mood, anxiety, depression, and brain fogginess. Too much serotonin causes paranoia, which is the feeling that you are being threatened.

3. Adrenaline

This messenger increases your heart rate and supplies oxygen to your muscles to fight or run from a threat. You feel the rush of adrenaline when you are late or about to miss your plane.

4. Endorphins

Endorphins are a natural painkiller and give you a euphoric sense. Laughter and aerobic exercise such as jogging or cycling promote the release of endorphins. Low levels of endorphins cause headaches and increase the risk of depression.

We will set our focus on serotonin because it plays an important role in influencing your prefrontal cortex and promoting your self-control.[10] A good amount of serotonin helps to support your prefrontal cortex. Insufficient serotonin reduces the effectiveness of your prefrontal cortex. This also explains why depressed people are more prone to aggression, which is the ramification of low self-control.

It is important that you maintain a sufficient amount of serotonin every day to maximize your self-control effectiveness. The normal range of serotonin level in blood is 101-283 ng/mL (nanograms per milliliter). Pay attention to this value during your routine blood test or health check.

The following list includes common offenders that lower your serotonin level:

1. Caffeine

After tea, coffee is the world's most consumed beverage in the modern lifestyle. Be aware of the lowered serotonin level it causes if you always rely on coffee to get through the day. Caffeine gives you a temporary quick burst of energy, followed by caffeine crash that leaves you with lassitude. Caffeine stimulates your brain activity into an overdrive mode to give you the enhanced focus. When the effect wears off, your fatigue increases to compensate for the extended resources used earlier.

Consuming about 350 mg of caffeine or more (three to five cups of brewed coffee) every day creates a dependence on it. When you abstain from caffeine, you will experience withdrawal symptoms such as headaches, irritability, depression, nausea, or painful muscles after about half a day. These withdrawal effects diminish after about a week.

	Caffeine content per serving (in mg)
Coffee	140
Energy drink	80
Expresso	80
Matcha tea	70
Chocolate	55
Black tea	47
Green tea	36
White tea	24
Decaf coffee	8

Caffeine Content in Various Beverages

Consider reducing caffeinated beverage intake to avoid developing dependency on caffeine and serotonin reduction.

2. Stress

Studies have proven that the level of serotonin decreases in response to stress.[11] Chronic stress exacerbates the problem by weakening the prefrontal cortex and strengthening the primitive brain.[12] Thus, stressful people exhibit lower self-control.[13]

Stress also increases appetite, even if you are not hungry. It is a defense mechanism that you need to stock up more calories to increase your preparedness for threats. People who are stressful tend to overeat.

Stress is inevitable in the daily life. You cannot eliminate all the stressors in life, but you can control how you face the stresses and implement a stress-management lifestyle to help ease them. Handling your stress is crucial to prevent your brain from growing into the state of chronic anxiety. It is evolving every moment based on the stimulus you feed it with. This experience is called neuroplasticity. If you constantly feel stressful, you face a higher risk of developing depression.

3. Alcohol

A short-term consumption of alcohol increases the serotonin level. A study found an increased amount of serotonin after a single drinking session.[14] However, when you consume alcohol regularly, your body builds tolerance and attempts to slow the release of serotonin.[15] A study shows that alcoholics have a lower level of serotonin compared to non-alcoholics.[16]

Alcohol also suppresses the activity of the prefrontal cortex.[17] You may have witnessed many violent and potentially dangerous events caused by drunkards. When you are drunk, you temporarily lose the ability to make good decisions, withhold your emotion, and make rational assessments.

After just one or two drinks, the impairment to the brain is detectable, but it is restored soon when you stop drinking. The damage to the brain is worse when you drink alcohol heavily. Studies show that chronic drinking damages the prefrontal cortex's function.[18] It develops serious and persistent change in the brain.

Fortunately, it is still possible to recover from the addiction after about a year of alcohol abstinence. Avoid alcohol as much as possible if you would like to maintain a healthy brain, keep your liver happy, and stay out of trouble.

4. Nicotine

Similar to the effect of alcohol, nicotine from cigarettes releases serotonin in the brain, causing a mood-boosting sensation in smokers for a short duration.[19] As you smoke regularly, your brain down-regulates the serotonin secretion and represses its production.[20] Scientists believe that the production can be reduced by as much as half.

5. Sleep deprivation

Studies have proven that when you are sleep-deprived for a night, your serotonin level increases.[21] This is the natural process to make you sleepy and encourage you to catch some sleep. As you continue to deprive yourself of sleep after a week, your serotonin production reduces, because your body would have adapted to your sleep deprivation routine and reduced its serotonin production to keep its level within the normal range. Its production remains low, even when you start to get adequate sleep. It takes a full one week of good sleep to normalize your serotonin production.[22]

There are a few methods to increase serotonin:

1. Diet

Serotonin cannot be obtained from any food. However, an essential amino acid from food, *tryptophan*, can help your body to manufacture serotonin.

	Tryptophan amount per kg of food (in gr)
Spirulina	9.3
Cod fish	7
Soybeans	5.9
Parmesan	5.6
Pork	2.5
Turkey	2.4
Beef	2.3
Salmon	2.2

Tryptophan Amount in Food

The amount of tryptophan in our body is typically quite low. The recommended daily intake of tryptophan for adults is 3.5-6 mg per kilogram of body weight.[23] If you weigh 55 kilograms, your recommended daily intake of tryptophan is 192.5-330 milligrams.

A diet high in protein limits the serotonin production, because when you eat a high-protein meal, more amino acids will be present in your bloodstream. Tryptophan has to compete with other amino acids in your blood to be absorbed.

Note: Amino acids are the compounds that form protein. When you consume protein food, the food is broken down into amino acids. Your body then uses the amino acids as protein to repair and grow your body tissues. There are twenty different amino acids, out of which nine are essential amino acids that your body cannot produce, and can only be consumed from food. They are histidine, leucine, isoleucine, lysine, phenylalanine, methionine, tryptophan, threonine, and valine.

To get around the problem when tryptophan needs to compete with other amino acids, you should balance your meal with carbohydrate food when eating tryptophan-rich food.[24] Consuming a carbohydrate meal triggers insulin production, which can help to carry the amino acids into your muscle cells. That way, tryptophan has a higher chance to be carried across your brain to manufacture serotonin.

2. Supplement

If you cannot obtain sufficient tryptophan from diet, introducing supplements to your food intake helps. The specific supplement to increase serotonin is 5-HTP and tryptophan. However, it is easy to over-consume serotonin if you are not careful with the dose. This could lead to a potentially life-threatening condition. Please consult your doctor before experimenting with any serotonin-targeting supplements.

3. Sunlight

A study discovered that the level of serotonin in the brain is higher during summer and spring than it is during winter and fall.[25] Sunlight is a natural antidepressant because of its ability to trigger more serotonin production. People often experience low mood, lethargy, and sadness during winter, or when spending more time indoors. A few minutes of sunlight exposure in the morning is good enough to lift your mood. Using a bright light therapy device can be a great alternative when you have no access to sunlight.

Note: A bright light therapy device mimics the brightness of sunlight. You can use the device for the treatment of circadian rhythm disorder. That is, your body does not know when it is time to sleep and when it is time to wake up.

4. Exercise

Serotonin produced during exercise makes you feel good after the session is over. People with a low serotonin level usually have no mood to exercise. Going for an exercise reverses the situation. It increases the serotonin level, which then uplifts your mood.

There are two types of exercises: aerobic exercise and anaerobic. Aerobic exercise uses the continuous supply of oxygen to sustain the workout. Examples of aerobic exercise are jogging, cycling, swimming, etc. Anaerobic exercise requires a higher amount of oxygen than aerobic exercise does, and during the shortage of oxygen, it uses the glycogen from the muscle cells as fuel to withstand the exercise. Examples of anaerobic exercise are strength training, sprinting, etc.

Both types of exercise help with serotonin boost, although aerobic exercise increases it more. A study shows that an increased amount of serotonin in the brain is associated with the fatigue during aerobic exercise.[26] Scientists discovered too that this effect diminishes to base level within one week when you discontinue exercising.[27]

That said, anaerobic exercise has its role in serotonin boosting too. It increases the uptake of amino acids in the bloodstream, which reduces the competition for tryptophan to be transferred to the brain. Pick one (or more) of the exercise types you enjoy the most to optimize adherence.

5. Cranial Electrotherapy Stimulation (CES)

CES is a non-invasive clinical treatment for people who suffer from anxiety, insomnia, and depression. The device delivers pulsed electrical currents to the brain to induce the state of relaxation. There is a good deal of evidence that shows increased serotonin production following a CES session.[28]

Although the device is expensive, it is a more economical way compared to long-term drug treatment. The best part is, the side effects of CES are very mild and self-limiting. Some people reported experiencing headaches or skin irritation after going through the session.

NEXT, we will discuss how to *detect* an imminent temptation that drains your willpower.

4

DETECT WEAKENED WILLPOWER

 No man is free who is not master of himself.

— Epictetus

You want to be able to detect when your willpower is declining so you can take an immediate action to replenish it, or stay away from the possible temptations or from making silly decisions. Failing to detect the ebbing of your willpower causes you to continue to immerse yourself straight into the situation that further drains and challenges your willpower. This often leads to willpower failure, and you lose the capability to use the rational side of your brain.

There are some subtle signs that surface when your willpower is low, but they can be difficult to notice if you are not mindful.

- Your heart rate goes up
- Your emotional reaction intensifies
- Your cravings grows stronger
- You try to avoid making any decision
- Simple things seem to be harder for you now

You should evade any important decision-making when you notice that your willpower is low. If this happens in the evening, relaxing yourself for a good night's sleep is a perfect idea. However, if you have already depleted your willpower in the middle of the day, take a break before you use your willpower again, or take a quick nap if you did not have a good night's sleep the previous night.

Although you cannot precisely measure the state of your willpower, you can at least quantify it in your stress response. Whenever you use your willpower to restrain something, your body generates stress. Everyone is stressed when he/she can't eat their favorite pizza. When you are stressed, your sympathetic tone rises.

Note: Sympathetic tone is one of the two divisions of the autonomic nervous system in our brain. It is a fight-or-flight response triggered in the face of danger. It is activated when the body receives a stress signal, and your brain encourages you to either face the danger or run away from it for your survival. The other division is parasympathetic tone, which is a rest-and-digest response that is more active when you are calm. When the sympathetic tone is raised, your parasympathetic tone reduces, and vice versa.

When your sympathetic tone rises, your heart rate increases and does not fluctuate much. This is indicated with heart rate variability (HRV) being low. On the other hand, when your parasympathetic tone rises, your heart rate decreases and fluctuates up and down. This is indicated with high HRV.

Measuring HRV allows you to know immediately if you are battling stress—which uses your willpower. High HRV means low stress and low willpower consumption. Low HRV means high stress and high willpower consumption. If you are keen on getting to know your HRV numbers, you can use a heart monitoring gadget that can measure HRV in real time.

Even with this, you cannot accurately determine if your willpower is low. This simply tells you that you are depleting your willpower to face the stress. It does not mean that your willpower is already hitting low. However, with this metric, you know that you are currently drawing your willpower.

If you catch yourself drawing your willpower continuously for a prolonged period of time, you can immediately find a way to stop your willpower from being perpetually drained. The obvious way is to remove the temptation completely. Removing the temptation does not restore your lost willpower; it only stops it from being further drained.

It is not always possible to eliminate the temptation. For example, you could be at a birthday party that is filled with the smell of pizza, which drains your willpower nonstop. In this case, an expedient measure might be to escape from the scene or ensure you are stocked up with willpower before joining the party. You can increase the HRV by manipulating the sympathetic tone response, which can be achieved by performing a slow breathing exercise. You can indeed increase your HRV, and restore a little of your willpower, but that does not discard the temptation that is still draining your willpower continuously.

WE HAVE ALREADY COVERED how to reduce your willpower consumption and replenish it. You have saved tons of willpower usage from unnecessary use. You have maximized it for your job, and you still have a lot of spare willpower when you get home. What can you do with that? Exercise it. Similar to our body muscle, our willpower will lose its effectiveness if you don't use it at all. In the next chapter, we will look into how to invest willpower to ***increase its reserve.***

5
____

INCREASE WILLPOWER RESERVE

> Well, I must endure the presence of a few caterpillars if I wish to become acquainted with the butterflies.
>
> — Antoine de Saint-Exupéry, *The Little Prince*

Increasing your willpower gives you the edge to get even more tasks done. To raise your willpower level, you need to use and challenge your willpower.[1] Faced with everyday temptations, if you succeed at fronting any challenge, you earn a little willpower out of it. The more willpower you use, the greater the increment you will get. The less willpower you use, the less increment you will get.

Let's assume you are trying to resist the same food every day. In practice, you will sometimes face a harder challenge, and sometimes an easier challenge. You may face a harder challenge when:

- Your spouse eats your favorite pizza while you are fasting
- Your cupboard is stocked with your usual go-to potato chips

You may have easier challenges when:

- Your spouse is fasting too
- There is no distracting food near you

Here, the willpower you earn back is slightly **more** on a difficult day, and slightly **less** on an easy day.

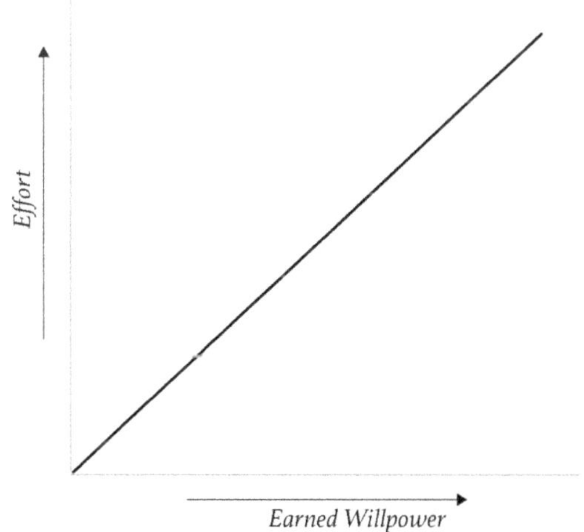

Effort vs. Earned Willpower

When you first attempt to quit smoking, you will spend a lot of willpower to resist cigarettes and ignore your craving. Over time, repeated successful attempts to stop smoking strengthens your willpower, and you eventually stop smoking with ease. Of course, this is not a linear progression that eases gradually; there are peaks and valleys when the withdrawal symptoms kick in, or when the environment cues are triggered.

You shall note that the effect wears off when you repeatedly challenge the same tasks. Successfully quitting junk food for 100 days does not grant you back 100 times the willpower you get when you succeed in quitting for one day. Every time you successfully overcome the same challenge, the willpower reserve increment decreases, as you get used to the same challenge. The result is, the willpower needed to handle the same challenge decreases too because it becomes easier and easier for you.

Surely, you can also deliberately set up your own challenge to train your willpower, such as:

- Watching a delicious food review hours after your last meal when you are fasting
- Placing your favorite donuts on the table when you are trying to eat clean

Even though you will gain some extra willpower when you succeed, you face a higher risk of succumbing to the temptations when you fail. I don't suggest doing this for the sake of increasing your willpower, and you should not do this to reduce your willpower consumption because the result will be disappointing. Companies spend big money to hire the best advertising creators who craft persuasive commercial advertisements and replace it with the new one when needed. You may have successfully reduced your willpower consumption to zero by challenging your temptation to the same pizza advertisement for 100 days, but when the company rolls out a new set of advertisements, it is a new challenge for you too, and you are back to square one; you are no longer immune to the pizza advertisement.

The willpower that you earn from resisting a certain thing is localized. If you train your willpower to be resistant of one thing, it does not mean it will be resistant of others. You may be resilient at resisting impetuous spending, but not chocolate. Attempting to challenge your willpower by confronting the willpower trap not only wastes your precious willpower but also is an infinite journey that does not lead to your better self. Let's discuss better alternatives that give you better odds at sticking to your routines, and more benefits other than just the extra strength of willpower. If you are trying to build new habits, I suggest starting with any of these, because not only will they spill the benefits over to other areas of your life but also they will help you increase your willpower to beget more good habits.

Physical Exercise

Scientists found that people who regularly exercise increase gray matter in their brain.[2] Gray matter is the neuronal cells components in the brain, and distributed at the surface of all brain regions, including prefrontal cortex. We have learned earlier that strong prefrontal cortex creates strong willpower. High volume of gray matter in your prefrontal cortex region is favourable for your willpower.[3]

Starting and maintaining an exercise regimen is always hard, and it's tiring for your willpower. This may even be the routine you are trying to build your willpower for. Every time you drag yourself to go to the gym, you draw a lot of willpower. Once you can maintain an exercise routine, and you begin to find exercise enjoyable, you naturally use less willpower just to get your body to exercise, but that does not mean that you will get less willpower trained in return. Instead of gaining the willpower increase from motivating yourself to exercise, you now gain willpower from the effort exertion during exercise.

When you spend effort to lift heavier weight, even when your muscles implore you to stop, you train your willpower. When the weight becomes too light for your muscles, you increase the weight to add challenge to your body. That new challenge also trains your willpower. When you bring yourself to run harder than the day before, you train your willpower. Therefore, exercise can be considered perpetual willpower training to keep both your body and willpower in shape. Don't go overboard with physical exercise for the sake of earning more willpower; otherwise you may end up overtraining or injuring yourself. On the other hand, when you are training with low exertion or low intensity all the time, you train less willpower.

Any form of physical exercise works to improve your willpower. You'd be better choosing one(s) that you find enjoyable.

Mental Exercise

Another way to strengthen your willpower is to exercise your mind. Playing cognitive-demanding games, such as Dual N-Back Memory, trains your brain.[4] Dual N-Back Memory is a simple game, but it challenges your focus. To win the game, you need to remember the sequence of letters and positions presented, and identify whether the letter or position is the same as the one that appeared before. When you lose focus, you lose the game. When you beat the game, the difficulty increases. This way, you can progressively train your focus.

Any other games work too, as long as they are aimed toward training your focus. Some high-tech games were developed with sensors placed on the scalp of your head to measure your brain activity and provide feedback on your game display. You gain score by maintaining focus. If you drift away, the sensor will detect it and you lose points.

There is only so much time that you have in a day, and you don't have to spend your time performing many mental exercises. Choose one you like best and move on with your life.

Willpower Limit

Cognitive neuroscientists once believed that the prefrontal cortex develops late in childhood. However, recent findings demonstrate that the environment after birth may shape the development of the prefrontal cortex in infants, which could be as early as the first year.[5] The intimacy of the parent-child relationship, good nutrition, and a good living environment favorably influence a child's brain development.

On the other hand, the following situations hinder children's prefrontal cortex growth:

1. Maltreatment, child abuse

Child abuse is a traumatic experience, and it causes adverse development of the prefrontal cortex. [6]

2. Poverty

Studies suggest that a family with low socioeconomic status exposes higher risk for children to an environment that is prone to neglect and malnutrition. [7]

3. Premature birth

The brains of premature infants are not as developed as those of full-term infants. Infants born at a gestational age between 32 and 36 weeks with no complication are also subjected to risk of impaired prefrontal cortex development, albeit at a smaller scale. The problem is worse for children who are born very premature at 27 weeks or fewer. [8]

Note: Gestational age is the period between conception and birth. Infants are considered premature if they are born before 37 weeks.

It is disheartening and unjust to children who need to face these circumstances. Fortunately, prefrontal cortex is trainable, and these children still have the opportunity to improve their prefrontal cortex as they grow up.

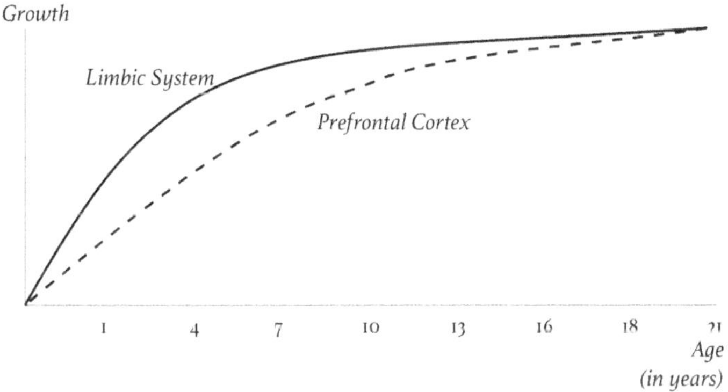

Limbic System and Prefrontal Cortex Development

Source: Casey et al., 2008

The limbic system is developed much earlier, while the prefrontal cortex isn't fully developed until we reach our mid-20s.[9] That is why younger kids are more impulsive, have less self-control, and are more risk-taking. Couple these with a lot of other things that they face—from their adolescent roller-coaster emotional state, first love, physiological changes, and integrating with unfamiliar social situations—and it makes them look like recalcitrant kids. They are not. It's just that they have not completed the development of their prefrontal cortex, while their primitive brain dominates their lives. Parents who understand this biological journey can help their children ride through the confusion that adulthood brings.

In 1990, psychologists conducted a Marshmallow Experiment on 32 children three to five years old to measure their self-control. The experiment was to give the child participants an option of either one marshmallow now or two marshmallows later.[10] Some children chose one marshmallow, and some waited for two marshmallows. The experimenters followed the children as they grew up, and what they discovered was fascinating. Children who chose two marshmallows were better at money management, exercised more, had a lower likelihood of obesity, were less stressful, and achieved higher SAT scores. The experiment famously concluded that children who can delay gratification for future rewards tend to lead a better life. This observation is bewildering because children at three to five years old are still developing their prefrontal cortex. Were they really already able to analyze the better future reward by waiting longer, or was it something else? Perhaps the children simply did not like to eat marshmallows, or they did not trust adults who promise to reward more if they waited longer.

Researchers at the University of California, San Diego revisited this experiment in 2020 on over 900 children of various socioeconomic populations, and parents' education.[11] It turns out that there is no supportive correlation between the ability to wait for the second marshmallow and long-term success. Toddlers of well-to-do families likely don't mind waiting for the second marshmallow, compared to those in poorer families. The former can rely on getting more marshmallows when they get home, while the latter may risk not seeing a marshmallow again if they decide to wait. This experiment illustrated that children at a tender age who do not wait for better rewards are not failures. They still can train their self-control as they grow up when their prefrontal cortex matures.

There is no conclusive study on whether there is any ceiling limit of willpower. But there is no need to endeavor the pursuit of unlimited willpower. If you have been training your willpower, at some point in your life, you may have accumulated a high capacity of willpower. That does not mean that you should stop when you reach that point. Continue to practice your willpower to maintain its strength.

To maintain resilience to temptation, anyone should train to strengthen their willpower regardless if they think they already have strong willpower. After all, there is no simple way to quantify the amount of willpower you currently have. Everyone has different motivation, capability, and habits. We have learned that when you exert higher effort, you use higher willpower. Difficult things demand higher effort. A thing that is difficult for you may be a cinch for others and vice versa. Therefore, two persons performing the same exact tasks every day do not necessarily mean they both have the equivalent amount of willpower. One may be left with exhausted willpower at the end, and the other may still have some spare willpower after completing all the tasks.

We all know that the methods parlayed to increase willpower reserve are good not just for your willpower but also for your mind and body. However, under real-life conditions, it is a vexing problem to implement them. One of them may happen to be your New Year's resolutions. When you are short on willpower, you will not intentionally challenge your willpower to increase it. The amount of willpower to be invested for your willpower training is always heavy. If you have a day job, you may plan to invest your remaining willpower after work to allow yourself to still perform your best at work. The best approach is always to form what you need to do as habits slowly in order to reduce the willpower consumption.

You should exercise your willpower with care. You don't want to get excited to increase it by introducing many new routines and overload it too much that you have no spare resources to face real temptations. Once you curb off an extensive amount of unnecessary willpower use in your daily life, you should amass more reserve to integrate these into your habits.

IN THE NEXT CHAPTER, we will look into how we can better *handle any relapse.*

HANDLE RELAPSE

 A man should control his life. Mine is controlling me.

— RUDOLPH VALENTINO

YOU MAY HAVE KNOWN SOME PEOPLE WHO, AFTER BREAKING THEIR diet rule once, continue to engorge more since they think they have already blown their diet; or a gambling addict who, after losing some money, continues to take their whole savings to gamble because they have already lost so much; or a smoker trying to quit who, after giving in to one cigarette, proceeds to smoke even more, since they have already damaged their lungs.

Let's discuss a strategy to handle any relapse so you don't aggravate the problem after failing.

What's happening here is that after having their willpower weakened, they give in to the temptations. They subsequently feel guilty or ashamed about giving in. These negative feelings further suppress your willpower, and they cause their primitive brain to continue to reign victorious and get you to surrender to your temptations even more. The more you feel that you are guilty, the more difficult it is for your prefrontal cortex to bring you back to your logical consciousness.

Depending on the severity of the things you have given in, paradoxically, the way to handle relapse is to be shameless and guilt-free. When you have lost control and eaten that forbidden donut, absolve yourself of your guilt and get on with your life.

Consuming a donut is not as devastating to your weight as you may imagine. Let's do some math here. A piece of chocolate donut contains about 334 calories. To gain just one pound of fat, you need to eat approximately 3,500 calories above your current maintenance calorie requirement. Let's assume your maintenance calorie requirement is 2,200 calories. This means in a day you must eat 3,500 + 2,200 = 5,700 calories (over two days' worth of your usual food intake) just to gain one pound of fat. Eating 5,700 calories a day is very difficult for most people.

Note: Maintenance calories are the amount of calories your body needs to remain at the same weight. Consuming calories above your maintenance calorie requirement makes you gain weight, while eating calories below your maintenance calorie requirement makes you lose weight.

You may wake up on the next day and be freaked out by the additional four pounds displayed on your scale. You do not actually gain that four pounds overnight. The extra weight results from the temporary water and food weight in your body, which is normalized after a few days. To gain four pounds, you need to eat approximately 22,800 calories in a day, which is pretty much impossible. For a comparison, here's the list of average calorie intake for different athletes.

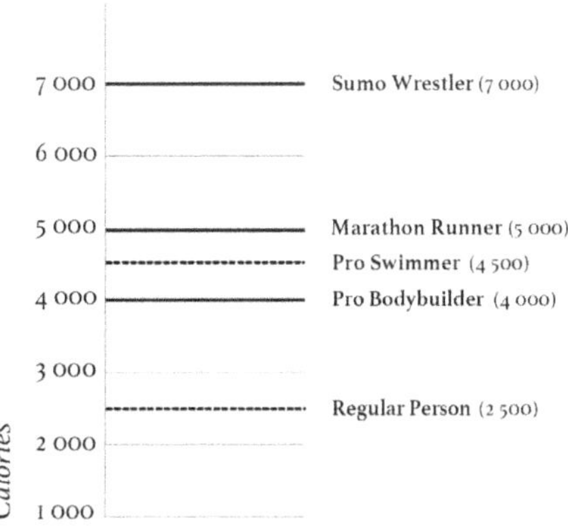

Approximate Calorie Intake per Day by Different Athletes

Be kind to yourself, enjoy your donut, and get back on track. Doing so eases your willpower usage, and you will less likely blow up your diet into a donut buffet.

The bigger issue arises if the problem is more severe, such as cheating on your spouse. Repairing the damage is going to take more than just forgiving yourself, and I have no solid solution for that.

We NOW HAVE COMPLETED ALL the core information needed to optimize your willpower. The next chapter merges all the information into a workable daily willpower planning.

DAILY WILLPOWER PLANNING

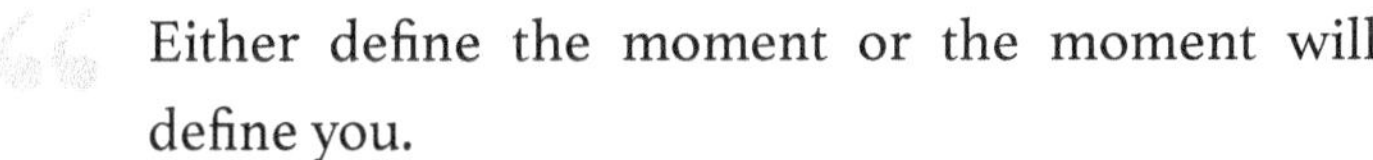

Either define the moment or the moment will define you.

— WALT WHITMAN

MOST PEOPLE TRY TO APPLY THE SEA OF ADVICE LEARNED FROM self-help books without consciously planning their willpower use. This makes it harder to comply with the suggestions in the books, as most of their willpower is wasted away in unnecessary matters. In this chapter, we will look into planning your willpower use daily. Let's begin with killing the willpower waste. It is crucial that you identify your current willpower wasters and trim them off to the absolute necessary. Be honest with yourself on matters that suck your willpower and remove them one by one, starting with the biggest one. They could be:

- Clutters on your desk
- Potato chips pack behind your transparent cupboard's window
- Unneeded notices from your multiple credit cards
- Irrelevant email subscriptions that do not matter to you
- Inessential app notifications from your phone
- Tangling multiple charging cables that confuse you when you need to charge
- Unimportant decision making

These will take time to do, but they form an important prelude to the steps that follow. Once these are cleared, let's plan your willpower use throughout a day. As you go on, and realize new unnecessary willpower waste, eliminate them.

1. Always strive to start with a full willpower tank

Make it a priority to get a good night's sleep so you can start every day with a full willpower tank. Build a consistent sleeping schedule to make sure you get enough sleep daily. You want to maximize your self-control daily, including weekends.

2. Order your tasks strategically

When you have options, always work on the most important task first before working on your less important tasks. If you have two tasks that are equally important, start with the most demanding one. But if both of them are demanding, take a brief break after finishing one task to replenish your willpower for the second task. When you have a very important event for the day that requires high willpower, exert as little use of willpower as possible beforehand, to devote the energy for the event.

3. Reduce as much willpower consumption as possible

Throughout the day, expose yourself to as few temptations as you possibly can, and structure your time with the least possible distraction, at least until after you have used your willpower for what's needed for the day.

- No social media
- No TV news
- No shopping
- No online browsing

4. Use the remaining willpower to build a new good habit, break bad ones, and increase your willpower reserve

Without changing your habits for the better, your life will remain the same. Set up a schedule to build a new good habit and break bad ones only when you know that you don't need to spend much willpower on that day, or there is no upcoming important task that you must fulfill, typically at the evening or during weekends. You don't want to exhaust your whole willpower when you still have some important matters to attend to. Whenever the time fits you, schedule your day to exercise, or do a mind training to increase your willpower reserve and keep its power in shape.

THIS ROUTINE SHOULD HELP you maximize your willpower usage every day. The biggest challenge generally occurs during weekends. Most people squander a lot of willpower on weekends by sleeping in late, partying, or binge-watching TV shows. These are pleasurable activities, but these likely will make you more anxious about yourself. The weekend is the most useful time to do something productive for yourself. Because you don't have to spend your willpower for your weekday job, you can at least channel your willpower for your own goals.

It is true that you deserve to pamper yourself during weekends after working hard during the workdays, and I agree we should not live like a machine to constantly seek to be productive. However, instead of exhausting all your willpower just for fun alone during the weekend, if you could at least use part of it to work on something important to you when your willpower is full, you would speedily progress your goals in your lifetime.

CONCLUSION

You have now completed the last chapter of the book. Learning to save a lot of willpower is of no use if you don't use it for your long-term goal. By all means you can just rest on your couch and lock yourself in an isolated place to avoid all possible temptations, but this is certainly not something that you want in life, nor a life worth living. At the same time, you don't need to design your lifestyle free of any indulgence. Balanced living that includes some indulgence is useful for your mental health and makes you happier. Extreme living on either end is miserable.

Recognize that it is nature's intention of even the most sensible person on the planet to get angry at their spouse, luxuriate, or succumb to binge eating when his/her prefrontal cortex is overworked.

- If your calm spouse just returned home late from work

and snapped at you, give him/her a hug for the hardship he/she endured at the office.

- When you have an appointment with a sales agent in the evening, and you already had a rough day, postpone the meeting to the next day to avoid making a bad financial decision.
- If you have an important matter that requires high mental energy to attend to, conserve your willpower as much as possible beforehand.
- When your young children display impulsive behaviors, realize that they are not screw-ups; nature has not completed their prefrontal cortex development yet.
- When your friends who are trying to slim down fail, don't label them as lazy. They could have worked extremely hard but their willpower is constantly drained by their environment.
- Even if it sounds relaxing, taking a break in a shopping mall is not as revitalizing as walking in a park.

It is inevitable that we face the challenge of willpower in this modern world. Instead of running away from it, let's use these strategies to our advantage. As a matter of fact, the higher you climb the social status ladder, the more vulnerable you are to willpower failure because the number of possible temptations increases, the demanding tasks required of you increase, and the need to handle your ego increases. You should not use this knowledge of exhaustible willpower as a license to cheat on your spouse and harm your marriage, or to get aggressive toward others. Ignoring to work on your willpower as you raise your social rank is irresponsible not only to yourself but also to your family and people around you.

Forewarned is forearmed. I hope this book will save you from ludicrous mistakes and help you make smarter choices in using your willpower. By now, you should have realized that you too can build any habit you dreamed of having. It is not a privilege that is admitted to just the few chosen ones.

Thank you for reading the book.

KEEP IN TOUCH

If this book benefits you, would you please take a moment to write a review? I would love to read your comments. It makes my day knowing that the years of willpower I've poured into completing this book could improve your life.

Keep in touch with me at said@saidhasyim.com.

If you wish to be notified of my next book update or special promotion, sign up to my mailing list at https://www.saidhasyim.com.

For a limited time and while stocks last, access the bonus material at https://www.saidhasyim.com/peak-self-control-exclusive if you purchased this book.

ALSO BY SAID HASYIM

ABOUT THE AUTHOR

Said Hasyim is a certified IT project manager with an obsession for finding the best ways to maximize his productivity. After more than a decade of arduous self-experimentation and research into bio-hacks, Said discovered various methods to improve his productivity. Now, he hopes to share his findings with his readers in his *Peak Productivity* book series to unleash their inner potential.

Find out more about Said at www.saidhasyim.com.

facebook.com/SaidHasyimReal

instagram.com/SaidHasyimReal

linkedin.com/in/saidhasyim

NOTES

Introduction

1. Statista. (2019, January 8). *Share of Americans who stuck to their 2018 New Year's resolutions.* https://www.statista.com/statistics/953562/share-of-americans-who-stuck-to-their-new-year-s-resolutions/
2. *Lack of willpower may be obstacle to improving personal health and finances.* (2012). American Psychological Association. https://www.apa.org/news/press/releases/2012/02/willpower

1. What Is Willpower?

1. Cheung, T. T. L., Gillebaart, M., Kroese, F., & De Ridder, D. (2014). Why are people with high self-control happier? The effect of trait self-control on happiness as mediated by regulatory focus. *Frontiers in Psychology, 5,* 1. https://doi.org/10.3389/fpsyg.2014.00722
2. Baumeister, R. F., Bratslavsky, E., Muraven, M., & Tice, D. M. (1998). Ego depletion: Is the active self a limited resource? *Journal of Personality and Social Psychology, 74*(5), 1252–1265. https://doi.org/10.1037/0022-3514.74.5.1252

2. Reduce Willpower Consumption

1. Nordgren, L. F., Harreveld, F., & Pligt, J. (2009). The restraint bias: How the illusion of self-restraint promotes impulsive behavior. *Psychological Science, 20*(12), 1523–1528. https://doi.org/10.1111/j.1467-9280.2009.02468.x
2. *Can polling location influence how voters vote?* (2008, June 1). Stanford Graduate School of Business. https://www.gsb.stanford.edu/insights/can-polling-location-influence-how-voters-vote
3. Statista. (2020, February 26). *Daily social media usage worldwide 2012-2019.* https://www.statista.com/statistics/433871/daily-social-media-usage-worldwide/
4. Urberg, K. A., Değirmencioğlu, S. M., & Pilgrim, C. (1997). Close friend and group influence on adolescent cigarette smoking and alcohol use.

Developmental Psychology, *33*(5), 834–844. https://doi.org/10.1037/0012-1649.33.5.834

5. Christakis, N. A., & Fowler, J. H. (2007). The spread of obesity in a large social network over 32 years. *New England Journal of Medicine*, *357*(4), 370–379. https://doi.org/10.1056/nejmsa066082

6. Graham, A. L., Papandonatos, G. D., Cha, S., Erar, B., Amato, M. S., Cobb, N. K., Niaura, R. S., & Abrams, D. B. (2016). Improving adherence to smoking cessation treatment: Intervention effects in a web-based randomized trial. *Nicotine & Tobacco Research*, ntw282. https://doi.org/10.1093/ntr/ntw282

7. Northwestern University. (2015, January 28). Dieters who make more connections in online weight-loss communities lose more weight. *ScienceDaily*. Retrieved December 9, 2020 from www.sciencedaily.com/releases/2015/01/150128141926.htm

8. Barrera, M., Jr, Chassin, L., & Rogosch, F. (1993). Effects of social support and conflict on adolescent children of alcoholic and nonalcoholic fathers. *Journal of personality and social psychology*,*64*(4), 602–612. https://doi.org/10.1037//0022-3514.64.4.602

9. Statista. (2018, May 31). *Cigarette smoking rate in Great Britain 2000-2012.* https://www.statista.com/statistics/289313/cigarette-smoking-penetration-rate-in-great-britain/

10. Rich, J. J. (2020, February 21). *FDA's grotesque cigarette warnings images are ineffective, have been found unconstitutional in the past.* Reason Foundation. https://reason.org/commentary/fdas-grotesque-cigarette-warnings-images-are-ineffective-have-been-found-unconstitutional-in-the-past/

11. Naomi Mandel and Steven J. Heine (1999). *"Terror management and marketing: He who dies with the most toys wins,"* in NA – Advances in Consumer Research Volume 26, eds. Eric J. Arnould and Linda M. Scott, Provo, UT: Association for Consumer Research, pp. 527-532.

12. Klein, Lawrence R. and Ozmucur, Suleyman. (2002). "Consumer behavior under the influence of terrorism within the United States," *Journal of Entrepreneurial Finance and Business Ventures*: Vol. 7: Iss. 3, pp. 1-16.

13. Masicampo, E. J., & Baumeister, R. F. (2011). Consider it done! Plan making can eliminate the cognitive effects of unfulfilled goals. *Journal of Personality and Social Psychology*, *101*(4), 667–683. https://doi.org/10.1037/a0024192

14. Iyengar, S. S., & Lepper, M. R. (2000). When choice is demotivating: Can one desire too much of a good thing? *Journal of Personality and Social Psychology*, *79*(6), 995–1006. https://doi.org/10.1037/0022-3514.79.6.995

15. American Psychological Association. (2012, December 1).*What you need to know about willpower: The psychological science of self-control.* http://www.a-

pa.org/topics/willpower

16. Bellet, Clement, De Neve, Jan-Emmanuel, and Ward, George. "Does employee happiness have an impact on productivity?" (October 14, 2019). Saïd Business School WP 2019-13. Available at SSRN: https://ssrn.com/abstract=3470734 or http://dx.doi.org/10.2139/ssrn.3470734

17. Stice, E., Burger, K., & Yokum, S. (2013). Caloric deprivation increases responsivity of attention and reward brain regions to intake, anticipated intake, and images of palatable foods. *NeuroImage, 67,* 322–330. https://doi.org/10.1016/j.neuroimage.2012.11.028

18. Karlan, Dean, Zinman, Jonathan, & Gine, Xavier. (2009). "Put your money where your butt is: A commitment contract for smoking cessation." *American Economic Journal: Applied Economics.* 2. 213-35.

19. Foxx, R. M., & Brown, R. A. (1979). Nicotine fading and self-monitoring for cigarette abstinence or controlled smoking. *Journal of Applied Behavior Analysis, 12*(1), 111–125. https://doi.org/10.1901/jaba.1979.12-111

20. Lally, P., van Jaarsveld, C. H. M., Potts, H. W. W., & Wardle, J. (2009). How are habits formed: Modelling habit formation in the real world. *European Journal of Social Psychology, 40*(6), 998–1009. https://doi.org/10.1002/ejsp.674

21. Webb, T. L., & Sheeran, P. (2008). Mechanisms of implementation intention effects: The role of goal intentions, self-efficacy, and accessibility of plan components. *British Journal of Social Psychology, 47*(3), 373-395. https://doi.org/10.1348/014466607x267010

3. Replenish Willpower

1. Gailliot, M. T., & Baumeister, R. F. (2007). The physiology of willpower: Linking blood glucose to self-control. *Personality and Social Psychology Review, 11*(4), 303–327. https://doi.org/10.1177/1088868307303030

2. DeWall, C. N., Deckman, T., Gailliot, M. T., & Bushman, B. J. (2010). Sweetened blood cools hot tempers: physiological self-control and aggression. *Aggressive Behavior, 37*(1), 73–80. https://doi.org/10.1002/ab.20366

3. Marks, V. (2005). Hypoglycaemia: Accidents, violence and murder. Part 1. *Practical Diabetes International, 22*(8), 303–306. https://doi.org/10.1002/pdi.854

4. Weiss, D. C. (2011, April 20). *A judge's full belly is good news for criminals, study finds. ABA Journal.* https://www.abajournal.com/news/article/a_judges_full_belly_is_-good_news_for_criminals_study_finds/

5. Weinshall-Margel, K., & Shapard, J. (2011). Overlooked factors in the analysis of parole decisions. *Proceedings of the National Academy of Sciences, 108*(42), E833. https://doi.org/10.1073/pnas.1110910108

6. Gailliot, M. T., Baumeister, R. F., DeWall, C. N., Maner, J. K., Plant, E. A., Tice, D. M., Brewer, L. E., & Schmeichel, B. J. (2007). Self-control relies on glucose as a limited energy source: Willpower is more than a metaphor. *Journal of Personality and Social Psychology, 92*(2), 325–336. https://doi.org/10.1037/0022-3514.92.2.325

7. Vadillo, M. A., Gold, N., & Osman, M. (2016). The bitter truth about sugar and willpower. *Psychological Science, 27*(9), 1207–1214. https://doi.org/10.1177/0956797616654911

8. Sanders, Matthew, Shirk, Steven, Burgin, Chris, & Martin, Leonard. (2012). The gargle effect: Rinsing the mouth with glucose enhances self-control. *Psychological Science.* 23. 10.1177/0956797612450034.

9. Chambers, E. S., Bridge, M. W., & Jones, D. A. (2009). Carbohydrate sensing in the human mouth: effects on exercise performance and brain activity. *The Journal of Physiology, 587*(8), 1779–1794. https://physoc.onlinelibrary.wiley.com/doi/10.1113/jphysiol.2008.164285

10. Vlaev, I., Crockett, M. J., Clark, L., Müller, U., & Robbins, T. W. (2017). Serotonin enhances the impact of health information on food choice. *Cognitive, Affective, & Behavioral Neuroscience, 17*(3), 542–553. https://doi.org/10.3758/s13415-016-0496-2

11. Temel, Y., Helmy, A., Pinnock, S., & Herbert, J. (2003). Effect of serotonin depletion on the neuronal, endocrine and behavioural responses to corticotropin-releasing factor in the rat. *Neuroscience Letters, 338*(2), 139–142. https://doi.org/10.1016/s0304-3940(02)01392-7

12. Arnsten, A. F. T. (2009). Stress signalling pathways that impair prefrontal cortex structure and function. *Nature Reviews Neuroscience, 10*(6), 410–422. https://doi.org/10.1038/nrn2648

13. Cell Press. (2015, August 5). How stress can tweak the brain to sabotage self-control. *ScienceDaily.* Retrieved December 9, 2020 from www.sciencedaily.com/releases/2015/08/150805140245.htm

14. LeMarquand, D., Pihl, R. O., & Benkelfat, C. (1994). Serotonin and alcohol intake, abuse, and dependence: Clinical evidence. *Biological Psychiatry, 36*(5), 326–337. https://doi.org/10.1016/0006-3223(94)90630-0

15. Pandey, S. C., Davis, J. M., & Pandey, G. N. (1995). Phosphoinositide system-linked serotonin receptor subtypes and their pharmacological properties and clinical correlates. *Journal of psychiatry & neuroscience: JPN, 20*(3), 215–225.

16. LeMarquand, D., Pihl, R. O., & Benkelfat, C. (1994b). Serotonin and alcohol intake, abuse, and dependence: Clinical evidence. *Biological*

Psychiatry, 36(5), 326–337. https://doi.org/10.1016/0006-3223(94)90630-0

17. Abernathy, K., Chandler, L. J., & Woodward, J. J. (2010). Alcohol and the prefrontal cortex. *International Review of Neurobiology*, 289–320. https://doi.org/10.1016/s0074-7742(10)91009-x

18. Schacht, J. P., Anton, R. F., & Myrick, H. (2012). Functional neuroimaging studies of alcohol cue reactivity: A quantitative meta-analysis and systematic review. *Addiction Biology*, *18*(1), 121–133. https://doi.org/10.1111/j.1369-1600.2012.00464.x

19. Bach, H., Arango, V., Kassir, S. A., Dwork, A. J., Mann, J. J., & Underwood, M. D. (2016). Cigarette smoking and tryptophan hydroxylase 2 mRNA in the dorsal raphe nucleus in suicides. *Archives of Suicide Research, 20*(3), 451–462. https://doi.org/10.1080/13811118.2015.1048398

20. Breitinger, H.-G. A., Geetha, N., & Hess, G. P. (2001). Inhibition of the serotonin 5-HT3 receptor by nicotine, cocaine, and fluoxetine investigated by rapid chemical kinetic techniques†. *Biochemistry, 40*(28), 8419–8429. https://doi.org/10.1021/bi0106890

21. Elmenhorst, D., Kroll, T., Matusch, A., & Bauer, A. (2012). Sleep deprivation increases cerebral serotonin 2A receptor binding in humans. *Sleep, 35*(12), 1615–1623. https://doi.org/10.5665/sleep.2230

22. Roman, V., Walstra, I., Luiten, P. G., & Meerlo, P. (2005). Too little sleep gradually desensitizes the serotonin 1A receptor system. *Sleep, 28*(12), 1505–1510.

23. Richard, D. M., Dawes, M. A., Mathias, C. W., Acheson, A., Hill-Kapturczak, N., & Dougherty, D. M. (2009). L-tryptophan: basic metabolic functions, behavioral research and therapeutic indications. *International Journal of Tryptophan Research*, 2, IJTR.S2129. https://doi.org/10.4137/ijtr.s2129

24. Wurtman, R. J., Wurtman, J. J., Regan, M. M., McDermott, J. M., Tsay, R. H., & Breu, J. J. (2003). Effects of normal meals rich in carbohydrates or proteins on plasma tryptophan and tyrosine ratios. *The American Journal of Clinical Nutrition, 77*(1), 128–132. https://doi.org/10.1093/ajcn/77.1.128

25. Praschak-Rieder, N., Willeit, M., Wilson, A. A., Houle, S., & Meyer, J. H. (2008). Seasonal variation in human brain serotonin transporter binding. *Archives of General Psychiatry*, *65*(9), 1072. https://doi.org/10.1001/archpsyc.65.9.1072

26. Davis, J. M., Alderson, N. L., & Welsh, R. S. (2000). Serotonin and central nervous system fatigue: Nutritional considerations. *The American Journal of Clinical Nutrition, 72*(2), 573S-578S. https://doi.org/10.1093/ajcn/72.2.573s

27. Dey, S., Singh, R. H., & Dey, P. K. (1992). Exercise training: Significance of regional alterations in serotonin metabolism of rat brain in relation to

antidepressant effect of exercise. *Physiology & Behavior*, 52(6), 1095–1099. https://doi.org/10.1016/0031-9384(92)90465-e

28. Gunther, M., & Phillips, K. D. (2010). Cranial electrotherapy stimulation for the treatment of depression. *Journal of Psychosocial Nursing and Mental Health Services*, 48(11), 37–42. https://doi.org/10.3928/02793695-20100701-01

5. Increase Willpower Reserve

1. Muraven, M. (2010). Building self-control strength: Practicing self-control leads to improved self-control performance. *Journal of Experimental Social Psychology*, 46(2), 465–468. https://doi.org/10.1016/j.jesp.2009.12.011

2. Erickson, K. I., Leckie, R. L., & Weinstein, A. M. (2014). Physical activity, fitness, and gray matter volume. *Neurobiology of Aging*, 35, S20–S28. https://doi.org/10.1016/j.neurobiolaging.2014.03.034

3. Schmidt, L., Tusche, A., Manoharan, N., Hutcherson, C., Hare, T., & Plassmann, H. (2018). Neuroanatomy of the vmPFC and dlPFC predicts individual differences in cognitive regulation during dietary self-control across regulation strategies. *The Journal of Neuroscience*, 38(25), 5799–5806. https://doi.org/10.1523/jneurosci.3402-17.2018

4. Colom, R., Martínez, K., Burgaleta, M., Román, F. J., García-García, D., Gunter, J. L., Hua, X., Jaeggi, S. M., & Thompson, P. M. (2016). Gray matter volumetric changes with a challenging adaptive cognitive training program based on the dual n-back task. *Personality and Individual Differences*, 98, 127–132. https://doi.org/10.1016/j.paid.2016.03.087

5. Schwartz, M. L., Rakic, P., & Goldman-Rakic, P. S. (1991). Early phenotype expression of cortical neurons: Evidence that a subclass of migrating neurons have callosal axons. *Proceedings of the National Academy of Sciences of the United States of America*, 88(4), 1354–1358. https://doi.org/10.1073/pnas.88.4.1354

6. Bick, J., & Nelson, C. A. (2015). Early adverse experiences and the developing brain. *Neuropsychopharmacology*, 41(1), 177–196. https://doi.org/10.1038/npp.2015.252

7. Johnson, S. B., Riis, J. L., & Noble, K. G. (2016). State of the art review: Poverty and the developing brain. *PEDIATRICS*, 137(4), e20153075. https://doi.org/10.1542/peds.2015-3075

8. Griffiths, S. T., Gundersen, H., Neto, E., Elgen, I., Markestad, T., Aukland, S. M., & Hugdahl, K. (2013). fMRI: Blood oxygen level–dependent activation during a working memory–selective attention task in children born extremely preterm. *Pediatric Research*, 74(2), 196–205. https://doi.org/10.1038/pr.2013.79

9. Rubia, K., Overmeyer, S., Taylor, E., Brammer, M., Williams, S. C. R., Simmons, A., Andrew, C., & Bullmore, E. T. (2000). Functional frontalisation with age: Mapping neurodevelopmental trajectories with fMRI. *Neuroscience & Biobehavioral Reviews, 24*(1), 13–19. https://doi.org/10.1016/s0149-7634(99)00055-x

10. Shoda, Y., Mischel, W., & Peake, P. K. (1990). Predicting adolescent cognitive and self-regulatory competencies from preschool delay of gratification: Identifying diagnostic conditions. *Developmental Psychology, 26*(6), 978–986. https://doi.org/10.1037/0012-1649.26.6.978

11. Kiderra, I. (2020, September 9). "The marshmallow test revisited." Medical Xpress. https://medicalxpress.com/news/2020-09-marshmallow-revisited.html